International Federation of Library Associations and Institutions
Fédération Internationale des Associations de Bibliothécaires et des Bibliothèques
Internationaler Verband der bibliothekarischen Vereine und Institutionen
Международная Федерация Библиотечных Ассоциаций и Учреждений
Federación Internacional de Asociaciones de Bibliotecarios y Bibliotecas

IFLA Publications 60

Nonchemical Treatment Processes for Disinfestation of Insects and Fungi in Library Collections

by Johanna G. Wellheiser

K·G·Saur
München · London · New York · Paris 1992

IFLA Publications
edited by Carol Henry

Recommended catalog entry:
Nonchemical Treatment Processes for
Disinfestation of Insects and
Fungi in Library Collections /
by Johanna G. Wellheiser
under the auspices of the IFLA
PAC Core Programme
München, London, New York, Paris: K. G. Saur, 1992
VIII, 118 p., 21 cm-
  (IFLA Publications; 60)
  ISBN 3-598-21788-9

Die Deutsche Bibliothek – CIP-Einheitsaufnahme

**Nonchemical treatment processes for disinfestation of insects
and fungi in library collections** / ed. by Johanna G. Wellheiser. -
  München ; London ; New York ; Paris : Saur, 1992
  (IFLA publications ; 60)
  ISBN 3-598-21788-9
NE: Wellheiser, Johanna G. [Hrsg.]; International Federation of Library
  Associations and Institutions: IFLA publications

Printed on acid-free paper
The paper used in this publication meets the minimum requirements of American National
Standard for Information Sciences - Permanence of Paper for Printed Library Materials, ANSI
Z3948-1984

Druck/Printed by Strauss Offsetdruck GmbH, Hirschberg
Binden/Bound by Buchbinderei Schaumann, Darmstadt

ISBN 3-598-21788-9
ISSN 0344-6891 (IFLA Publications)

ACKNOWLEDGEMENTS

This work was made possible by the International Federation of Library Associations (IFLA) and by the Council on Library Resources under the auspices of the Robert Vosper IFLA Fellows Programme. The Metropolitan Toronto Reference Library (MTRL) generously supported the research by providing interloan, word processing and other administrative services.

My gratitude goes to all of the people who contributed their enthusiasm, patience, time and expertise. I would like to acknowledge the encouragement and support provided by Frances Schwenger (Director, MTRL) and Margaret McGrory (former Assistant Director, MTRL), as well as Elizabeth Beeton (Assistant Director, MTRL), who came to the project at midpoint.

Particular thanks are due to: Merrily Smith (IFLA Preservation and Conservation Core Programme Director) for her guidance throughout the project; Tom Parker (President/Entomologist, Pest Control Services Inc.) and Karen Turko (Head, Preservation Services, University of Toronto) for their hours of draft review and wise counsel; and Tom Strang (Sr. Assistant Conservation Scientist, Canadian Conservation Institute) for his assistance and advice on many occasions.

I am also grateful to Mary-Lou Florian (now retired Chief, Conservation Services, Royal British Columbia Museum), Karen Furgiuele (Technical Advisor, Gardex Chemicals Ltd.) and Nieves Valentin (Coordinator, Scientific Investigation, Instituto de Conservación y Restauratión de Bienes Culturales) for providing information and answering questions.

Special appreciation is also due a number of individuals at MTRL including Dawn MacMaster for doing the lion's share of the word processing with a smile, and Karen Lenk and Ann Douglas (Assistant Conservators) for their assistance and persistence in tracking down elusive references and proofreading.

In spite of all the help received from these and other sources, I want to emphasize that the statements made and the views expressed in this publication remain the responsibility of the author. Also that the inclusion of a product or service does not constitute its endorsement. Finally, a salute to my tolerant husband.

PREFACE

The purpose of this report is to examine the principles, practices and development of nonchemical treatment processes for disinfestation of insects and fungi in library collections. It focuses on paper-based materials because they remain the predominant format in our care. The processes described are mainly, but not exclusively, those that would be suitable for the mass treatment of collections. Many of the methods do have application for smaller scale situations.

This report is written for the individuals responsible for the preservation of collections in their library. The placement of this responsibility varies from institution to institution, and may include preservation librarians and administrators, collections managers and conservators. It is assumed that the reader would have an understanding of fundamental preservation and conservation principles. While the report is not primarily intended for archivists, curators and records managers, many of the issues for their respective institutions are very similar to those faced by libraries.

This report is not intended as a step-by-step guide for use in the event of an infestation. Rather, its intention is to outline the characteristics of the various processes currently available or under development, to discuss issues relating to process evaluation, selection and application, to indicate where information is tentative or incomplete and to outline areas of future research.

This report addresses an issue which concerns all libraries. It is for all individuals and institutions who take a serious professional interest in disinfestation treatments that are safe, effective and affordable.

TABLE OF CONTENTS

1.0   EXECUTIVE SUMMARY

The perspective on disinfestation of library collections is rapidly changing. A decade ago the majority of libraries used chemical pesticides, primarily fumigants. Subsequently, growing concerns over the use and effect of fumigants have resulted in re-evaluation and changes in treatment strategies. The reasons for such change relate mostly to issues of human health and safety. However, mounting evidence of the damaging effects of chemical treatments on collection materials has also played a key role in these decisions.

In recent years, there has been increased focus on the prevention and control of infestation through the use of integrated pest management approaches. Concurrent with this trend, there has been increased activity towards the development of alternative means of pest eradication in collections. Given that libraries require safe and effective methods that are appropriate to the nature and scale of their problems, as well as their resources, it is likely that no one process will prove to be a panacea. However, a number of the alternative processes described have demonstrated considerable success to date and show enormous potential for a variety of applications.

The primary conclusions of the report are:

- Based on current knowledge, it is not possible to conclude that any of the processes have reached a stage of development that would conclusively meet all the criteria for safety (human and collection), effectiveness and economy. Of the alternative processes examined, freezing offers the most advantages and few disadvantages.

- Based on current knowledge, comprehensive comparative analysis of the processes is difficult. For instance, the treatment of certain types/sizes/formats of materials may be equipment specific rather than process specific.

- The technology of disinfestation overall is evolving at an increased pace.

- The preservation/conservation community is making increased and successful use of research from other fields of discipline.

- There is a pressing need for the published results of further evaluation and testing of the most promising methods.

- There is a pressing need for further documented experience of process(es) application by libraries.

Although the solutions to the problems of infestation will always be risk-benefit situations, it is encouraging that the current emphasis on human- and collection-benign treatment processes maximizes the benefits while minimizing the risks. It is also clear that these treatments must be employed in the context of other complementary measures, such as the maintenance of low temperature and relative humidity, and the systematic monitoring of collections.

2.0   INTRODUCTION

The problem of pest control is one that is faced by virtually all libraries. While infestation, in general, tends to be an ongoing issue in more tropical areas of the world, institutions in more temperate climates certainly are not immune. Collections are subject to damage, decomposition or destruction by a wide variety of pests, the most common being insects and fungi, and to a lesser extent rodents and other animals. The nature and complexity of this problem is now further complicated by the increased world-wide movement of books and other materials through purchase, gift and exchange programmes, as well as exhibition and inter-library loan. Materials are routinely shipped by train, truck, ship, airplane, etc. in a wide variety of physical and biological environments. Aside from the development of an infestation on-site in an institution, collections and/or packing materials may well become infested en route prior to acquisition. Insects, in particular, transported from one region/country to another can appear in greater numbers and prove to be more harmful and resistant than the resident species.

In the past, popular opinion was that the best method of eliminating pests was chemical. Pesticides, in various forms, were used because they were, in general, immediately and obviously effective, available, relatively simple to apply and in many cases, low in cost. It is now recognized that the use of chemical pesticides can result in damage to the very collections we seek to preserve and protect. Many studies now document clearly the damaging effects of many pesticides on the constituent materials of library collections. Moreover, frequent, uncontrolled and unnecessary use of chemicals poses unacceptable risks to human health and safety, and the environment. Accumulations of residues of toxic preparations and products of their decomposition can be immediately hazardous and remain so for many years.

The development of chemical resistance in pests also poses new challenges. For the repeated use of insecticides has led by means of simple natural selection to the evolution of resistant strains of many of the most important insect pests. Commercial insect pests have now evolved resistance to all major classes of insecticides including the most recent addition, the synthetic pyrethroids. Such resistance is not believed to apply widely to library insect pests now, except perhaps to cockroaches.

Not only do pests cause damage to collections and the facilities and buildings that house them, but they may also be dangerous to human health, in the form of infections, diseases and allergies. Clearly, safe and effective prevention programmes are needed. Also critical is the availability of safe and effective treatment processes, since no amount of planning can reduce the occurrence of infestation to zero.

In recent years, it has become recognized that the effectiveness of a treatment method is no longer the sole criteria for its selection. Many other factors must now be carefully considered. The process should be safe for the operator(s) of the equipment or facility, and the environment. As well, no harmful residues should remain in the collections that may later pose a risk to library personnel or users. The process should not change the chemical or physical properties of the treated materials or affect their natural ageing processes and it should be possible to treat items in their entirety. Ideally, no preselection should be necessary and it should also be inexpensive and rapid.

As collections are composed of a wide variety of constituent materials and formats, it is necessary to evaluate the effects of various methods before the selection of a process. This issue is increasingly problematic as there become available many more different types of papers, coatings and sizings, adhesives, and other binding materials. The problem of infestation is further intensified where collections are made from poor quality materials and items are deteriorated and fragile to start with.

Other fields of discipline such as the agriculture, health care, and food industry, etc., are also involved in pest control and their applications have proven very useful to the conservation and preservation community. There remains, however, a great and urgent need for information on the effectiveness, application and effects of different processes. Such knowledge is essential so that informed and responsible decisions can be made regarding treatment of collections. The library community must further promote and support the development of safe and effective pest treatment technologies and encourage their use, so that libraries may have available to them a collective knowledge base of experience and information applicable to the treatment of collections in their care.

3.0   AGENTS OF INFESTATION

3.1   INTRODUCTION

Insects and fungi are reviewed briefly in this section as background to the discussion of nonchemical treatment methods. Excellent and extensive information on the identification, characteristics and behaviour of insects and fungi is available in the literature. Such information, along with specialist advice, can assist in the prevention of infestation, identification of species and life stage, as well as in distinguishing between active infestation and items which are damaged but no longer contain living eggs, larvae or adults, or viable spores.

3.2   INSECTS

Insect species constitute the majority of living things on the earth. Estimates of insect species run as high as 6 million with the number of described beetles alone exceeding 500,000. Their aptitude for survival is strong: science and history have yet to record the disappearance of a single insect species. Their reproductive capabilities are prodigious: in 1984, the earth's insect population was estimated at one billion billion or 1,000,000,000,000,000,000 (Baur 1984).

Book eating/infesting insects are ubiquitous in temperate and tropical climates. While they can certainly be found in the heated facilities of colder climates, they mostly originated in semi-tropical and tropical areas. More than seventy species have been identified as enemies of library materials. Some are regular inhabitants and others come on an irregular basis from nearby, or in some cases, faraway materials or premises to infest collections.

All insects in their life-cycle go through a metamorphosis, a system of periodic moulting where growth proceeds in a series of steps until the adult stage is reached. Some insects, like beetles and moths, go through a complete metamorphosis - egg, larva, pupa and adult. Others, such as booklice and cockroaches, exhibit incomplete metamorphosis - egg, larva, nymph, and adult. It is generally the larva, while feeding, that causes the most damage to library and other materials. Adults eat little in comparison with the growing immature stages. Different species have different food requirements and some require different foods at different stages in their life cycle.

Of the species of insects that will infest library collections some, like cockroaches, are omnivorous. Other species are more selective and will attack only cellulose materials (paper, cardboard and textiles), starches (adhesives and book cloths) or protein materials (wool, parchment and leather). Most insects cannot readily digest cellulose and are attracted to collections by sizings, glues and starches. Other collection materials seemingly uninteresting to insects may in fact be vulnerable to attack. For example, in 1967 there appeared the first report of damage to colour slides by carpet beetle larvae (Cunha 1971).

Other insects will attack wood. Some start development in living timber and may subsequently emerge from objects made from infested wood, while others infest cut seasoned timber. The latter present the greatest hazard and include beetles which can be particularly destructive to collections, shelving, furniture and building structures. Larvae of some beetles take many years to develop and because they leave only a thin layer of surface wood, infestation may only be discovered after severe damage has already occurred.

Insects not only consume materials, but cause damage by their tunnelling, burrowing, nesting activities, body secretions and excrement. They are sometimes difficult to detect because they may attack from the back of shelving and bookcases through to the interior of books and boxed materials. Often insects are inconspicuous and seldom seen, unless their habitat is disturbed.

In general, the optimum temperature for the development and reproduction of insects is $20°$ - $30°$ C. As insects are unable to regulate their own temperature, at below $10°$ C they will become inactive as their metabolism is slowed. Death usually occurs when temperatures below $-20°$ C or above $45°$ C are achieved for a period of time. Most insects prefer a relative humidity (RH) of 60%-80%. There are many exceptions to these generalizations. For example, the firebrat prefers much warmer temperatures, $32°$ - $40°$ C is optimum (Parker 1988).

Insects also require moisture. Some species obtain water from the conversion of foodstuffs within the body, while others like silverfish require conditions of high relative humidity (75% - 97%). Humidity control can reduce problems with some species, especially those which are encouraged by development of fungi.

3.3   FUNGI

Of the microbiological agents, the fungi constitute the major risk for libraries. Other microorganisms such as bacteria, and actinomycetes can cause deterioration and decomposition of paper and other materials such as parchment, leather and plastics. However, instances of damage reported by libraries is most often caused by fungi. Conditions in libraries, as well as archives and museums, generally support the growth of fungi more than that of bacteria. This is because many fungi require less moisture for their growth than do other microorganisms.

Fungi, in popular terms mould and mildew, are abundant on the earth and every library certainly contains numerous genera and species. There are over 100,000 known living species of fungi, and perhaps another 200,000 species which have yet to be identified (Nyberg 1988). Fungi are extremely ecologically adaptive and once established tend to maintain their own microclimates. They participate in the decomposition of most natural materials, as well as man-made products. Certain fungi consume cellulose and cause irreparable damage to paper. Others attack a variety of the constituents of book materials including leather, glues, pastes and adhesives. Some fungi cause surface structural damage and/or discolourations, many in brilliant colours.

Constituent library materials vary widely in their resistance to mould growth depending upon their raw materials and their method of manufacture/production and storage. Fillers, coatings and sizings may be potential sources of nutrients. A slightly acid pH of about 5.5 is preferable, although fungi can vegetate in the pH range 1.4 to 10.0. Poor quality modern papers containing polymers, non fibrous material other than cellulose and impurities are especially conducive to prolific growth of microbial agents (Kowalik 1980).

Fungi absorb nutrients from dead or living organic matter as they are unable to generate their own organic compounds. The body of fungi called mycelium is composed of branching threads or hyphae. Reproduction occurs by means of spores carried on vegetative and generative parts produced by the hyphae.

The temperature range for optimal growth and reproduction is variable but is approximately 15° - 35° C. The average optimum temperature is often cited to be about 30° C, with a relative humidity of 75% to 100% (Wessel 1969). However, many species demonstrate a great tolerance of environment and can endure long periods of freezing or sub-freezing temperatures. Most species are less tolerant of an alteration of below- and above-freezing conditions. Others may tolerate a temperature of 100° C for as long as 25 years (Kowalik 1980, 105).

Relative humidity is important to the growth of fungi; however, it appears that the combination of RH and temperature is critical. It is generally agreed that below 70% RH there is little growth. Kowalik (1980) identifies the most suitable conditions as a temperature of 24° - 30° C and an RH of 65% - 80%.

Light is not considered to be an essential requirement for most fungi. In fact, ultraviolet light is injurious or lethal to some species. Some fungi show a great resistance to the action of the sun. In general, however, sunlight is harmful.

While many bacteria are anaerobic, most fungi require oxygen for growth. In addition, elements required include carbon, hydrogen, oxygen, nitrogen, sulphur, potassium and magnesium. Other trace elements and vitamins are also needed. Cellulose provides many of these elements and other nutrients can be found in leathers, pastes and adhesives. Other materials include paints and plastics. Dust, dirt and stains can also provide additional nutrients - cellulose material thus contaminated by human contact provides an excellent and necessary source of nitrogen (Brokerhof 1989).

Because the food range of fungi is so wide and spores exist everywhere, environmental control is critical. The literature cites quite a variety of recommendations for relative humidity and temperature. It is generally recommended that materials be maintained at a relative humidity of 50% - 55% and a temperature between 18° C and 20° C.

4.0   INTEGRATED PEST MANAGEMENT/ERADICATION

Thomas Parker aptly describes the appeal of collections to pests:

> Libraries and archives, where books, printed materials, manuscripts, maps, prints, photographs, and various other materials are stored, perused, and exhibited, are not unlike the setting in agriculture where huge quantities of foodstuffs are stored for long periods of time. The library setting is a concentration of foodstuffs, including starches, cellulose, and proteins, which form a banquet for insects, rodents, and mould. (Parker 1988, 7)

Libraries, as do archives, also provide almost limitless opportunities for pests that do not feed directly on collections, but may cause damage to the facility and furnishings, and attract other pests that do attack paper and books. Moreover, this inside environment is often luxurious when compared to the harsh extremes of the external climate. In such conditions, population explosions of various pests can and do occur.

There are no simple solutions to the prevention and control of pests in libraries, particularly where a maximum result is desired with minimum risk to the staff, public and the collections. Furthermore, in today's world of fiscal restraint, activities of a more visible and glamorous nature are often given priority. More difficult to achieve is support for a programme that is generally "behind the scenes" and may be viewed as unnecessary. In fact, the occurrence of insects and fungi is frequently only taken with any degree of seriousness in the event of a major and rampant infestation.

It is now generally acknowledged that a multi-faceted approach is necessary to maximize the usefulness of any pest control programme. The term integrated pest management (IPM) is used to embody the concept that all pest control programmes must rely on a number of compatible and environmentally sound methods and techniques to effect the desired result. Experience has shown that the problem of pests in libraries can be effectively and safely handled through the use of an IPM approach. (Parker 1988)

It has been suggested that IPM is inadequate to meet the particular requirements of libraries, archives and museums because IPM, having originated in the food industry, tolerates an acceptable level of infestation in the finished product. Rather, the goal of cultural institutions should be integrated pest eradication (IPE).

It is important to recognize that the complete eradication of all pests from a facility is not easily achieved. In the case of insects, there will likely always be a resident population; however, the goal of the control programme, whether termed IPM or IPE, must be to eradicate those insects that threaten the collections, either directly or indirectly. Spores of fungi will always be present, but active infestation can be prevented through environmental control and other measures, such as building maintenance and good ventilation.

IPM/IPE targets the sources of the problem by its concentration on excluding pests from a facility. This approach recognizes that total dependency on chemical control methods results in a typical response pattern where the pests or their damage is discovered, chemical treatment is applied and the problem is then considered solved until the next discovery of pests and their damage.

An IPM/IPE strategy focuses on continual awareness of potential problems and immediate response to infestations. The use of chemical solutions are considered to be a last resort and fumigation is used only when all other control measures have failed, and nonchemical treatments are not feasible or applicable. A combination of control techniques is utilized on a routine and concerted basis including insect traps, external facility modifications, control of moisture, cleanliness measures and inspection programmes. Such control requires 100% awareness by all staff, including contract personnel.

Collections in libraries may be valuable, unique and irreplaceable, either as artifacts or for their informational content. Other collections, while not unique, are extremely difficult and/or costly to replace. No information was found on the dollar losses suffered by libraries as a result of infestation. However, given the evidence of damages and losses documented in the literature and the reported costs for treatment and recovery operations, it is clear that IPM/IPE has a valuable role to play in the preservation of collections.

5.0   REVIEW OF COMMONLY-USED CHEMICAL TREATMENTS

5.1   INTRODUCTION

In spite of knowledge from the 19th century regarding the importance of environmental control and collections maintenance to the prevention of infestation, conservation has often focused its attention on the curative and remedial. This is particularly evident in the area of infestation where the advances in chemical technologies were applied with enthusiasm in libraries, as well as in archives and museums, for the purpose of pest control, particularly collection fumigation. Also, until fairly recently, information regarding identified problems from industrial, health care and agricultural applications was not widely known in the library community. For example, studies in the 1950s onwards confirmed that plastics retain ethylene oxide (EtO), some in quantities not desorbed for four or five months. In addition, the installation, operation and maintenance of fumigation chambers in libraries were often done without appropriate safety measures. At times this was the result of misinformation or ignorance. All too often, unsafe fumigation was undertaken in blatant disregard of existing legislation. Changes in legislation, registration, certification, etc. also meant that some continuing practices became illegal.

Between 1935 and 1965, the fumigants used in cultural institutions became less radical - museums, archives and libraries began to turn away from fumigants like hydrogen cyanide, ethylene chloride/carbon dioxide and methyl bromide. As well, the use of other compounds potentially harmful to human health became less frequent (Ballard and Baer 1986). These changes paralleled those that were occurring in the food and other industries where the principles of pest eradication and control were in the process of being evaluated and modified.

In 1980, a survey of U.S. libraries demonstrated a fairly uniform approach to fumigation - 35% were using a form of EtO and another 16% were planning an EtO facility. Subsequently, growing concerns regarding the use of EtO resulted in a significant shift in treatment strategies. This was demonstrated by an informal 1983 survey of fourteen U.S. libraries and archives where 36% were abstaining totally from fumigation, although previously 50% had used EtO (Ballard and Baer 1986)

Bell and Stanley's 1980 survey of pest control in museums presented a disconcerting picture of the use of chemical treatments and pest control in general. In spite of the reported use of methyl bromide, EtO, Dowfume 75®, carbon disulphide and other hazardous compounds over a third of the respondents took no safety precautions. Of this group, most felt that there was no health hazard and it was reported that the legality of the use of a particular pesticide was of little concern. Alternatives to chemical pest control were noted by only a few - heat treatment in cases, freeze-dry experiments and RH/temperature controls. (Bell and Stanley 1981)

There is now a broader and fuller recognition that pesticides effective against insects and fungi are toxic at varying levels to humans, and that they may be reactive with many of the collection materials to which they are exposed. Such knowledge in concert with changes in legislation, has led not only to the reappraisal of many commonly accepted and routinely undertaken pest control measures, but also to the development of alternative nonchemical treatment processes.

5.2   FUMIGATION

The most common method of mass eradication of insects and fungi is by fumigation, where infested collections are exposed to a lethal gas or vapour. There are three types of fumigants (based on physical state at room temperature when applied): gaseous, liquid and solid. Gaseous fumigants are the most hazardous and should only be used in chambers according to applicable legislation. Liquid fumigants evaporate to produce vapours. Solid fumigants are high vapour pressure crystals which convert to vapour with time, and some with heat. Advantages of fumigation can include effectiveness, good penetration, short exposure time, low per item cost and ability to treat multiple items at a time. Disadvantages of fumigation are the toxicity of the gases/vapours to the operators and the environment. In addition, residues remaining in the treated material may pose a health hazard to users of the treated material. Fumigants are known to damage certain constituent materials of collections and they do not provide residual protection against reinfestation.

Exposure to pesticides can produce health effects ranging from acute to chronic illness depending on the type of pesticide, the amount of pesticide, and the duration of exposure. Some of the most devastating consequences of exposure such as cancer may not surface until decades after initial exposure.

There are some similarities in the behaviour of the three types of fumigants: gaseous, liquid, and solid. Although fumigants, in general, are more toxic than pesticides, the gaseous fumigants are the most toxic of all. They enter the body primarily through inhalation although some ... also can be absorbed through the skin. Most liquid fumigants can be absorbed through the skin, but inhalation of their vapours is a more common entry route [Although less toxic to humans than gaseous fumigants, liquid fumigants may be chronic poisons (Parker 1988)]. Solid fumigants are the least toxic of the fumigants and are usually absorbed only through vapour inhalation ... fumigant gases, remain in the air and can easily spread through ventilation systems, open doors ... people at a distance. (Center for Safety in The Arts 1988, 129)

The determination of the relative hazard of fumigants is a complex task. Often, available information on substances is not directly comparable or specific information on a substance is sparse, incomplete or unavailable. A number of hazard rating systems exist, as do various animal toxicity test values, probable human lethal dose values, carcinogenicity ratings, exposure standards and recommended exposure limits. None alone provides a full human health hazard comparison.

For example:

- The U.S. National Fire Protection Association Hazard Identification System is intended to provide a general idea of the inherent hazards (health, flammability and reactivity) of a material and the order of severity of these hazards as they relate to fire protection, exposure and control. It is not designed to be used for comparative purposes. (Dean and Tower 1991)

- The Oral LD_{50}, Dermal LD_{50} and Inhalation LC_{50} tests for animal toxicity give a comparative 'indication' of the acute toxicity of a chemical in a strain, sex or age group of a particular animal species. The tests were neither designed or intended to provide information on long-term exposure.

- The U.S. Occupational Safety and Health Permissible Exposure Limit (PEL) is the eight hour time-weighted average legally enforceable standard. It cannot be used to determine relative toxicity because the basis on which the limits are established vary from substance to substance.

- The Threshold Limit Value (TLV) for the eight hour time-weighted exposure recommended by the American Conference of Governmental Industrial Hygienists (ACGIH) cannot be used in the comparison of materials because the basis on which values are established also vary from substance to substance. The same is true for the Short Term Exposure Limit (STEL) of the ACGIH for maximum exposure up to fifteen minutes. Note: TLVs are adopted in whole or in part by many countries and local administrative agencies throughout the world.

Clearly, it is essential to understand not only the purpose of each of the systems/values/standards, but also their limitations. It should also be noted that a rating system of any kind cannot take into account the specific hazards of specific work sites, that is, how a substance is handled and used, as well as the physical constitution of the individuals exposed to a particular substance, Furthermore, TLV, STEL, LD_{50}, etc. values are being steadily lowered as pesticide studies are completed. Thus, a review schedule for updating information and revising practices must be undertaken.

There does not now exist a universal or standardized toxicity rating scale. However, the U.S. Human Hazard Signal Word required on pesticide labels can provide some idea of relative toxicity and some measure of the hazard faced by the user. The requirements are outlined in Part 156.10 Labelling Requirements for Pesticides and Devices of the Federal Insecticide, Fungicide and Rodenticide Act (FIFRA). This legislation is regulated by the U.S. Environmental Protection Agency. Toxicity is based on five hazard indicators (Oral LD_{50}, Inhalation LC_{50}, Dermal LD_{50}, Eye Effects and Skin Effects). Labels are required to bear one of the following Signal Words according to the pesticide's toxicity category.

There are four Toxicity Categories for pesticides:

Toxicity Category	Signal Word	
I	"DANGER"	most toxic
II	"WARNING"	↓
III	"CAUTION"	↓
IV	"CAUTION"	least toxic

If a Category I pesticide is in Category I because of its oral, inhalation or dermal toxicity, the label must also carry the word "poison" and a skull and crossbones. The Signal Word "CAUTION" may refer to Toxicity Category III or IV, but if the label carries a precautionary statement, the pesticide would not be classified within category IV, the least hazardous of the categories (Russell 1988).

In Canada, similar legislation to that of FIFRA exists for the labelling (Precautionary Symbols and wording) of pesticides. The categories are defined by hazard - poison, flammability, explosive, corrosive and eye. The legislation covering this labelling, the Pest Control Products Act (Schedule 3, Registration Guidelines for Registering Pesticides and Other Control Products), is regulated by Agriculture Canada.

The U.S. FIFRA Human Hazard Signal Word (and the Canadian Precautionary Symbol) is end-use product-based. Therefore, the determination of the toxicity/hazard of active ingredients (versus specific products) is not necessarily straightforward.

Following is a brief review of the fumigants that have been commonly used for the disinfestation of library materials including information on their uses, chemical reactivity, physical properties, efficacy and toxicity. Other sources should be consulted for full detail on the characteristics, hazards and applications of each.

Note: 1. Unless otherwise indicated, the Human Hazard Signal Words (as determined by the Toxicity Category) provided are taken from the *Farm Chemicals Handbook* (Meister 1991). The pesticide dictionary in this publication is a compilation of experimental and commercial pesticides available in the U.S. and around the world. Discontinued products are also included for reference and are so designated.

2. The fumigants are listed in alphabetical order within the types (gas, liquid and solid) except where ortho-phenyl phenol is grouped with thymol, as they have both been commonly used for mould control.

5.3   GASEOUS FUMIGANTS

Gaseous fumigants are the most toxic of pest control chemicals. Based on the U.S. FIFRA Toxicity Categories, ethylene oxide (pure), methyl bromide, phosphine and sulphuryl fluoride are classified within Toxicity Category I (DANGER), the most hazardous of the categories. Hydrogen cyanide is not listed in the 1991 *Farm Chemicals Handbook* (See 5.3.2 Hydrogen Cyanide). Previously, hydrogen cyanide was reported to be classified within Toxicity Category I (DANGER) (Center for Safety in the Arts 1988). Ethylene oxide (mixture) is classified within Toxicity Category II (WARNING).

5.3.1.   ETHYLENE OXIDE

Ethylene oxide (EtO) began to be used as an agricultural insect fumigant in 1928, and by the 1980s was in common use in many cultural institutions. EtO, sold under its tradenames Oxyfume®, Carboxide®, etc., became a standard gaseous fumigant in libraries and is commonly used in a 10 or 12% concentration in a carrier gas of carbon dioxide (CO_2) or freon. Carboxide® is considered to be superior to Oxyfume® as the CO_2 sets up the insects for a lethal EtO dose. EtO, by itself, without freon or CO_2, is highly toxic, flammable in liquid form and explosive in its gaseous state.

EtO is effective against insects in adult, larval and egg stages, as well as fungi. Sterilization against bacteria can also be achieved. The efficacy of the dosage was considered to be 10 times greater than that of the available alternative, methyl bromide. However, in recent years the use of EtO has come under intensive scrutiny due to concern for safety of those handling EtO and EtO treated materials. As well, many questions have arisen regarding potential damage to the constituent materials of collections.

The U.S. Occupational Safety and Health Administration has determined that "EtO represents a carcinogenic, mutagenic, genotoxic, reproductive, neurologic and sensitization hazard to workers" (Ballard and Baer 1986, 144). Safety requirements for use and handling of the gas have become increasingly stringent. The threshold limit value (TLV) has been reduced worldwide. In the U.S. it is set at 1 ppm. Studies on the evacuation and rinsing of EtO in chambers and fumigated materials demonstrate that it is extremely difficult to achieve concentrations below the reduced TLVs (Residori and Ronci 1986). The use of EtO mixtures with freon as a carrier gas (Oxyfume®) is also problematic, in that freon is now considered to be one of the major causes in the reduction of atmospheric ozone.

With regard to the effects of EtO on collections, the literature cites many studies identifying a variety of changes, sometimes conflicting, in a variety of EtO-fumigated materials: the presence and persistence of EtO in plastics; the retention of EtO in materials containing fat and protein (parchment, leather, wool, etc.) and possible premature aging of proteins; an increase/decrease in the strength of EtO treated paper; and the increased sensitivity to microbial attack of EtO treated parchment, paper and microfilm (Florian 1987, 1988; Ballard and Baer 1986; Gallo 1978; Green and Daniels 1987; Valentin 1986). Aside from the obvious problem of damage that can be caused to materials by EtO treatment and the ethical question of permanently altering their chemical and physical properties, there remains the critical issue of the offgassing/desorption of EtO over time with its potential hazards to staff and users.

The European Community has prohibited (throughout the confederation) the use of EtO for all agricultural uses since December 31, 1990. It is unlikely that this ruling will cover cultural institutions (Postlethwaite 1991). Union Carbide, a major manufacturer in the U.S. no longer sells Oxyfume® or Carboxide® for use in museum chambers (Derrick et al. 1990). In Canada, EtO was registered for use at one time, but is now classified non-eligible.

5.3.2 HYDROGEN CYANIDE

Hydrogen cyanide (HCN) is an extremely fast-acting human toxin. It is particularly effective against insects but hardly at all against fungi (Brokerhof 1989) and has been used in libraries for disinfestation. It is reported to discolour some pigments and corrode metals at high humidities. The U.S. Center for Safety in the Arts recommends "do not use" and notes that the greatest number of poisonings have resulted from its use as a fumigant (Zycherman and Schrock 1988). Derrick et al. (1990) report it is not used in the U.S. as a fumigant. HCN is not registered for use in libraries or museums in the U.S. or Canada.

5.3.3 METHYL BROMIDE

Methyl bromide is a colourless, easily liquified gas having a chloroform-like odour. It is highly toxic by ingestion, inhalation or absorption through the skin. It has been widely used as a fumigant for wood-boring insects and also for the treatment of paper materials in museums, archives and libraries. Sold under the tradenames Brom-O-Gas®, Brozone®, Methogas®, etc., it is commonly used for the fumigation of insects and occasionally for fungi.

A major problem with its use is the production of disagreeable mercaptan-like odours when materials containing sulphur have been fumigated. The following is a partial list of materials that should not be fumigated with methyl bromide: leather goods, paper (cured by a sulphide process), photographic chemicals, woolens (especially angora), etc. (Dawson 1988)

Methyl bromide is not recommended by the Library of Congress Preservation Office for use on library materials, especially leathers, vellum, photographic films and prints (McComb 1983). Research has also indicated that methyl bromide reduces the physical strength of paper (Flieder 1969). Other effects noted have included the darkening of lead pigments, and the softening of natural resins and varnishes.

Methyl bromide is not registered for use in libraries in Canada. It has been used and is currently reported to be registered for use in the United Kingdom (Child 1988, 1991).

5.3.4 PHOSPHINE

Phosphine (hydrogen phosphide), sold under the tradename Phostoxin®, is a colourless, flammable, explosive gas generated by the reaction of aluminum phosphide with water or water vapour. It is an extremely mobile gas and is, if used appropriately, effective against insects in all stages of their life cycle. It is not effective against fungi or bacteria. In general, it is used commercially for the fumigation of grain and other foodstuffs, as well as the timber in buildings and furniture. Phosphine has been reported for use in museum applications (Fenn 1989, 1990; Child 1988).

This fumigant is reported to react with all metals (aluminum, brass, copper, gold, nickel, silver, steel, etc.), especially with copper, to cause extreme corrosion. Due to the known acute hazards of phosphine and the lack of adequate research on its chronic hazards or materials effects, it has been recommended that alternate methods of disinfestation be sought (Fenn 1990).

Phosphine is not labelled for use in U.S. libraries or museums, and it is not registered for use in Canada, although there is some latitude with one product where the labelling is open to interpretation. It is reported to be registered for use in the United Kingdom (Child 1991).

5.3.5. SULPHURYL FLUORIDE

Sulphuryl fluoride, sold commercially by the Dow Chemical company under its tradename Vikane®, is a colourless, odourless gas that is effective against insects, but it is a poor ovicide. Research indicates that Vikane® decreases the activity of some fungi and bacteria, but does not kill fungal spores.

Vikane® has excellent powers of penetration, low absorption characteristics and dissipates rapidly after aeration. It is stable and non-flammable under normal conditions. It is less toxic to humans than many fumigants; however, no studies on the long-term exposure effects of Vikane® have been undertaken.

Vikane® has largely been used as a structural fumigant for buildings, construction materials and furnishings. It has been also reported for use in cultural institutions (Hastings 1991). In a collaborative effort, the Getty Conservation Institute (GCI), the Canadian Conservation Institute, the Smithsonian Institution's Conservation Analytical Laboratory and the Dow Chemical Company have been studying the potential adverse effects of sulphuryl fluoride on materials found in museum collections and used in conservation. Also, a group at the University of Florida, through a contract with the GCI, is evaluating fumigant concentration. Preliminary results show that Vikane® does react with metals, cellulose and proteins. Future testing will incorporate differing fumigant concentrations at various humidities to determine the level of Vikane® that can be safely used on museum materials. (The Getty Conservation Newsletter 1988; Postlethwaite 1987; Derrick et al. 1990)

A recent report outlined the results of testing on a selection of materials, metals, pigments, resins, celluloses, proteins and dyes. Various chemical and physical changes were observed, some of which were attributed to acidic fumigant impurities. Fumigation with the impurities removed caused fewer changes (Baker et al. 1990).

5.4   LIQUID FUMIGANTS

There are virtually no liquid fumigants available today in the U.S. (Parker 1991{b}) or Canada. Most of these liquids have been found to be extremely hazardous to human health and safety, and questions have arisen as to their effectiveness. Carbon tetrachloride alone is briefly reviewed. Based on the U.S. FIFRA Toxicity Categories, carbon tetrachloride is now classified within Toxicity Category II (WARNING). Previously, this fumigant was reported to be classified within Toxicity Category I (DANGER), the most hazardous category (Center for Safety in the Arts 1988).

5.4.1.   CARBON TETRACHLORIDE

Carbon tetrachloride sold under the tradename Dowfume 75® (70% ethylene dichloride and 30% carbon tetrachloride) is a colourless liquid with an ether-like odour. Acute exposure has resulted in many fatalities (Center for Safety in the Arts 1988). It is a suspected human carcinogen and animal studies show damage to male and female reproductive systems. It is reported to dissolve waxes, lacquers and rubber and corrode metal at high humidities. Dowfume® is no longer available in the U.S. (Derrick et al. 1990). In Canada, the registered use of carbon tetrachloride as an insecticide was suspended in 1984.

5.5   SOLID FUMIGANTS

Based on the U.S. FIFRA Toxicity Categories, dichlorvos is classified within Toxicity Category I (DANGER) and its label must carry the word "POISON" plus a skull and crossbones.   Paradichlorobenzene is classified within Toxicity Category II (WARNING).

Ortho-phenyl phenol and thymol are not listed in the 1991 *Farm Chemicals Handbook*. The Gosselin, Smith and Hodge (1984) Toxicity Classes (Probable Oral LETHAL Dose, Human) for ortho-phenyl phenol are 4 (very toxic) and 3 (moderately toxic) respectively. These classes are done on a scale of 1 to 6 (6 is supertoxic).

5.5.1   DICHLORVOS

Dichlorvos, an organophosphate insecticide, has in the past been commonly used in cultural institutions in the form of insect strips (vapour phase insecticide), sold under the tradenames Vapona®, No Pest Strip®, DDVP®, Vaponite®, etc. U.S. National Cancer Institute tests are positive and it is a suspected human teratogen. It is reported that a recent NTP publication does "establish the carcinogenicity and mutagenicity of dichlorvos" and the Center for Safety in the Arts recommends against its use as "there is no safe level of exposure to carcinogens" (Babin 1990, 1).

Dichlorvos is reported to corrode metals at high humidities, dissolve some resins, glues and plastics and cause colour alterations in some dyes (Center for Safety in the Arts 1988; Stone and Edwards 1988; Dawson 1988). It is further reported that DDVP causes visible reactions with animal fats and oils, plant resins and various organic and inorganic compounds, as well as weight gains in many materials (Williams, Walsh and Weber 1989).

Due to a variety of circumstances, the dry resin pest strip was unavailable for a period of time. It is now sold in the U.S. under the name Pest Strip®. There are believed to be fewer long-term problematic effects on materials with the dry type of strip than with the wet strip. Dichlorvos is registered for use in libraries and museums in Canada and the United States. (Parker 1991{b})

5.5.2   PARADICHLOROBENZENE

Paradichlorobenzene (1-4, dichlorobenzene), commonly known as PDB is a colourless, solid (crystals or cake) at room temperature. It has been used extensively as an insecticide fumigant. It has a strong solvent action, softening adhesives and plastics and has been reported to discolour papers and other materials, including leather (Child and Pinniger 1987) and soften some plastics and resins (Center for Safety in the Arts 1988).

PDB is moderately toxic on inhalation and prolonged inhalation/ingestion can cause liver damage. Its reproductive effects are unknown, its carcinogenic effects are under investigation and it is not registered for use in museums in the U.S. (Center for Safety in the Arts 1988). Its registration in the U.S. is a controversial issue due to its use for other applications. PDB is registered for use in libraries and museums in Canada.

5.5.3   ORTHO-PHENYL PHENOL

Ortho-phenyl phenol (OPP) is a whitish crystal and has been commonly used by libraries for the control of mould. The use of OPP has been similar to that of thymol, although it is recommended for use in humidification chambers, impregnation of paper sheets and as a paste preservative, but not for fumigation (Nagin and McCann 1982).

OPP is slightly toxic, and acts as an eye and respiratory irritant. Prolonged and repeated exposure may lead to kidney damage. It is thought to be less toxic than thymol; however, it remains on the U.S. Environmental Protection Agency list of toxic chemicals due to the evidence on potential carcinogenicity, developmental toxicity and environmental persistence (Baer and Ellis 1988).

The fungistatic and fungicidal abilities of OPP appear to vary with the species of mould, the method of application, and the length of exposure. A recent study concluded that OPP (and thymol) were not very effective as fumigants. While each had the ability to stop or retard fungus growth, neither was totally effective in preventing germination of fungus spores (Haines and Kohler 1986).

5.5.4 THYMOL

Thymol (methyl-isopropyl-phenol) is a white crystal with a phenolic odour. It has often been used on library materials in its crystalline form from which a toxic vapour is produced by gentle heating. In a closed chamber, thymol can reportedly kill insects, fungi and spores providing there is adequate concentration and a long enough exposure time. Thymol has also been used in solution with organic solvents for fog/spray application, applied to paper strips that are then sealed with the materials to be treated and as a fungicide in starch pastes.

In recent years, questions have been raised as to the fungicidal action of thymol and the length of its effectiveness: thymol was observed as only partially effective in preventing the germination of fungus spores (Haines and Kohler 1986) and thymol in paper was not retained beyond 24 hours in standard museum storage conditions (Arney and Pollack 1980). Additionally, the use of thymol is not without risk to artifact materials. Damage has been observed as follows: softening of varnishes and resinous paints, damage to certain oil- and resin-based inks, embrittlement and buckling of parchment, recrystallization of thymol on the surface of artwork and the yellowing of acrylic sheeting and paper of artwork in frames.

Thymol acts as a skin, eye and respiratory irritant and is toxic by ingestion and inhalation. Studies indicate that exposure to its vapours can affect the circulatory and central nervous systems. It is reported that thymol is now considered a possible carcinogen (Ellis 1987). Exposure limits have yet to be established. Thymol is not registered for use as a fumigant in Canada, but as a material preservative and disinfectant.

5.6 OTHER

Napthalene has a long history of use in cultural institutions overall. It is not listed in the 1991 *Farmer Chemicals Handbook*. Previously, it was reported as being classified within Toxicity Category III-IV (CAUTION) (Center for Safety in the Arts 1988). The Gosselin, Smith and Hodge (1984) Toxicity Class (Probable Oral LETHAL Dose, Human) for napthalene is 3-4 (moderately toxic - very toxic). These classes are done on a scale of 1 to 6 (6 is supertoxic).

5.6.1 NAPTHALENE

Napthalene, commonly known as mothballs, is a colourless to brown solid with a mothball-like odour. It is really a repellant not a fumigant, that is, it is not designed to kill insects. Its effectiveness is questionable and it is considered a rather poor repellent of pests associated with textiles or fabrics (Center for Safety in the Arts 1988, Parker 1988). Its carcinogenic and reproductive effects are unknown.

Napthalene is reported to corrode some metals and soften some resins, and can recrystallize on specimens. However, Dawson's (1988) tests revealed no noticeable changes in a variety of materials (bubblepack, wool, silk, selected metals, etc.) exposed to napthalene. The more porous materials did retain the odour of napthalene for some time. In Canada, it is registered for use in libraries and museums.

6.0 NONCHEMICAL TREATMENT PROCESSES

6.1 INTRODUCTION

The use of nonchemical treatment processes for many applications is increasing world-wide. This trend is reflected in the conservation literature where reports and studies now document with considerable regularity the serious interest and intent to further develop and apply these methods to library situations. Evidence also clearly suggests that there are fewer and fewer libraries which can continue to justify the use of toxic fumigants, except in extraordinary circumstances. Libraries are also no longer operating in isolation from developments in related fields and are making use of the knowledge and experience of industrial, commercial and other applications.

The obvious immediate advantage of the nonchemical treatment methods is the absence of chemicals that pose hazards to human health and safety, and the environment, as well as cause unacceptable changes/damages to constituent materials of collections. While this implies a measure of assurance, there remains the need to evaluate these issues for nonchemical methods as well.

In a comprehensive assessment of the suitability of a particular process, it is necessary to consider a range of factors and their priority for the particular application:

Chemistry and physics of the process.
History of its use and state of advancement.
Effectiveness of the treatment.
Methods of process application.
Reliability of the process.
Material effects on books, single sheet materials, etc.
Flexibility for other materials and formats.
Hazard to human health and safety.
Environmental compatibility.
Economic considerations (capital and operating).
Availability of the process.
Impact on library operations.
Legal requirements.
Alternative process applications.

While it is unlikely that the "perfect" process does exist, criteria for the ideal situation can be outlined. The process would:

- Present no hazard to human health and safety short- or long-term. It would be safe for the operator of the equipment/facility. It would not use, create or release toxic or otherwise harmful chemicals or residues.

- Present no hazard to the environment. It would not release toxic or otherwise harmful emissions, residues, effluent, etc.

- Be effective and reliable in the treatment of library-infesting insects in all their life stages.

- Be effective and reliable in the treatment of library-infesting fungi in all developmental stages.

- Be recognized for use in the treatment of library collections. That is, development/advancement/experience with the process would be such that its mechanisms, operation and application are known and documented.

- Be non-damaging to the constituent materials of library collections. It would cause no negative change to their physical and chemical properties, nor affect their natural ageing properties.

- Require no or minimal preselection or pretesting.

- Allow materials of various types/sizes/formats to be treated in their entirety.

- Be flexible in its application so that equipment or facility changes could be made to suit specific institutional needs and resources.

- Require no or minimal pre-treatment and post-treatment procedures.

- Be able to be done in-house or readily available on a commercial basis.

- Require minimal monitoring in operation.

- Not require special certification/registration to meet applicable legislation/regulation.

- Have minimal effect on normal library operations.

- Require minimal staff training.

- Be low cost in terms of staff resources, equipment, maintenance, transportation, supplies, overhead, etc.

- Permit rapid turn around of collections.

6.2   LOW TEMPERATURE: DEEP-FREEZING

6.2.1   DESCRIPTION

The majority of insects that inhabit libraries and their collections originated in tropical and subtropical climates and many no longer exist except in areas of human habitation. The theory is that these insects have developed no naturally occurring mechanisms to protect them from freezing temperatures and are more vulnerable to rapid injury and death. Only those insects that have evolved in and adapted to cold climates have built up a tolerance to cold. There are exceptions however, and some insects demonstrate metabolic changes which allow them to survive low temperatures for various periods of time.

The rate of life processes in living organisms is slowed with a decrease in temperature. It has been reported that, in general, insects become inactive at $50°$ F [$10°$ C] (Story 1985) and that the activity of stored food insects is arrested at $15°$ C (Mullen and Arbogast 1984). Still lower temperatures can have a lethal effect. Research is not yet complete; however, freezing under appropriate conditions appears to be an effective method of library insect disinfestation and is reported for use by a number of institutions.

Freezing can be used as a method of retarding the growth and metabolic activity of fungi; however, it is not recognized as a method of disinfestation.

6.2.2   HISTORY OF USE

Freezing is, of course, used domestically and commercially for the storage of packaged food and food products in order to preserve flavour, nutrients and appearance while at the same time preventing spoilage and the development of infections. Freezing is used in the biological and medical sciences to preserve organs, tissues and cells. It has also been successfully used (in the form of freeze drying, etc.) for drying waterlogged materials.

Among the first to conduct scientific studies into the effects of low temperatures on various species of insects were Payne (1926) and Salt (1936). Interest in the use of low temperatures for insect eradication appears to have diminished after 1939 with the introduction of DDT and other broad spectrum insecticides (Ketcham 1984). Research into the practical application of low temperatures reappeared in the 1970s. Mullen and Arbogast stated in 1979 that "there is insufficient information available on time-temperature-mortality relationships to permit the application of low temperature as a control method". Since then, further research has been undertaken to examine treatment parameters and it is generally agreed that effective disinfestation can be achieved by deep-freezing.

Overall, there are few extensively documented cases in the literature on the use of freezing for the eradication of insects in cultural institutions. An outbreak of booklice was treated at the Herbarium in Queensland by flash freezing (Bruce and McGregor 1976) and wooden icon panels were reportedly successfully treated by freezing in an unheated location over the winter (Toskina 1978). It is reported that the University of Aarhus in Risskov, the Royal Botanic Garden at Kew, as well as Stockholm, the New York Botanical Gardens, the State Herbarium in Leyden and the Herbarium in Utrecht use deep-freezing to treat herbarium specimens (Brokerhof 1989; Crisafulli 1980; Cowan 1980). The Royal British Columbia Museum also treats herbarium specimens by deep freezing following a two day drying period (Florian 1986). The State Museum in Leyden regularly freezes its entire collection and all incoming specimens (Brokerhof 1989). Experiments have also been conducted for mammal collections and general museum pests. The Peabody Museum of Natural History has used deep-freezing for many years to preserve specimens (Nesheim 1984).

Libraries too have come to use freezing as an alternative to chemical means. Yale University's Beinecke Rare Book and Manuscript Library was in 1977 the first library to use deep-freezing to rid its collections of book-eating insects. Since then there have been few documented examples of the use of this method in libraries. Yale remains the best recorded case (Nesheim 1984). Yale continues to use this method as a preventive measure in the processing of new acquisitions. This technique for their application is considered 100% successful (Noack 1990).

The Law Library of the University of California, Berkeley, recently used freezing to treat an infestation of *Gastrallus pubens* Fairmaire. Circumstances of the infestation were similar to that of Yale in that it was a beetle from the same genus, vellum books were most affected and it was a cataloguing backlog that had permitted the infestation to gain a hold. The treatment will be considered a success if no adult beetles are found after a further two years. It was noted that two years may not be long enough - some species of larvae have been documented to live 11 years. (Boal 1990)

The Humanities Research Centre at the University of Texas used the deep-freezing technique to treat an incoming book collection infested with a variety of insects, predominantly dry-wood termites, as well as moths and cigarette beetles. The freeze disinfestation of approximately eighty cubic feet of material was considered to be successful. (Stewart 1988)

Experiences discussed with other institutions including the National Archives of Canada, the Royal British Columbia Museum, the Maine State Archives, the Newberry Library (Chicago), Columbia University, Milwaukee Public Museum, as well as that of the author's institution, the Metropolitan Toronto Reference Library, confirm the apparent success of this method. Disinfestation was reported as complete and no damage to collections was noted. There was reported in the literature, an instance where materials at the Swedish Museum of Natural History were found to be damp after two days of deep freezing. This phenomenon remains unexplained (Smith 1986).

6.2.3 PROCESS

In summary, the freezing process consists of five stages:

1. Pre-treatment procedures.
   Identification and documentation of nature and extent of infestation.
   Quarantine of infested collection.
   Bagging, sealing and boxing of materials where applicable.
   Maintenance of materials at room temperature.
   Transport of materials to in-house or external facility.
   Loading of materials in freezer. Allow for adequate air circulation.
   Placement of equipment, as required, to monitor/record the time/temperature parameters.

2. Freezer cool-down.
   Heat sources turned off to accelerate freezing rate.
   Desired freezing temperature is reached and maintained.
   Note: Rapid cool-down is desirable.

3. Exposure/Extermination.
   Desired freezing temperature is maintained.
   Monitor to verify and control time/temperature and equipment operation.

4. Recovery to room temperature.
   Defrost cycle is initiated where applicable.
   Temperature of freezer is slowly increased.
   If rate of temperature increase cannot be controlled, remove materials to refrigerator or cold storage.
   Remove materials from freezer/refrigerator/cold storage to quarantine area.
   Leave materials bagged and sealed until they have reached room temperature.
   Note: Slow thaw rate is desirable.

5. Post-treatment procedures.
   Determine effectiveness of treatment (reviving insects or new emergence).
   Examine and assess condition of materials.
   * Repeat cool-down, freeze-thaw cycle where necessary.
   Transport materials from external facility where applicable.
   Re-examine materials for treatment effectiveness.
   Quarantine further where necessary to monitor effectiveness.
   Remove insect remains, debris, etc. and leave material in bag if possible.
   Transport materials back to conditions of good storage.
   Complete documentation record.
   Adapt process where necessary.

Freezing can be readily undertaken in-house by an individual institution or on a co-operative basis with several participating organizations. Commercial freezing operations may also undertake this treatment. Requirements for the specific needs of a library application must be clearly understood by external operators.

6.2.4 REQUIREMENTS

6.2.4.1 Legislation

No legislation is known to exist regarding the in-house disinfestation of library materials by freezing. External freezing facilities that process food products are required to take certain measures when handling materials other than food.

6.2.4.2 Equipment/Facility

Thirty to forty cubic foot commercial chest freezers have been most commonly reported for use in the literature for the treatment of herbarium and museum collections. However, Yale (Nesheim 1984) uses a walk-in blast freezer with interior dimensions of 10 x 11 x 8 feet. A blast freezer is a standard quick-freeze food storage freezer with electric fans behind its freezing coils. These fans move the cold air generated by the coils around the interior at a rapid rate. Thus, materials loaded at room temperature (21° C) are brought to below freezing temperatures much more quickly than is possible with a conventional freezer. Yale's freezer was supplied by a local refrigeration company and modifications were made including a temperature recorder, recording thermocouples, a ground switch and smoke detector for the freezer's fan motors. Additionally, six stainless steel multi-shelf food service trucks with nine shelves and a non-skid ramp were purchased.

The Yale freezer uses Refrigerant R-502, an inert chlorofluorocarbon gas, and a refrigerant oil called Sunesco. Installation was done by the refrigeration company, electrical connection by the university and service on a contract basis is done by the supplier. This blast freezer has the ability to reach and hold -29° C to -32° C within four to five hours after loading and start up at normal room temperature of 21° C.

Smith reports the development and use of the Wei T'o® Book Dryer - Insect Exterminator, a modified commercial freezer, Hussman VML - 2BS two door supermarket-type freezer that provides approximately 40 cubic feet of interior space. The freezer was redesigned for use as an insect exterminator and for the purpose of salvaging water-wetted books. Modifications included engineering design, new components, electrical rewiring including the manufacture and installation of a custom-made control panel. The reasons for these changes for the purpose of insect extermination were to lower the minimum temperature achievable, and to provide more sensitive temperature controls and safety devices to protect books from damage. The control panel includes a high and low point temperature controller, a 12 point digital indicating thermocouple, a refrigeration cycle and defrost timer, a time delay switch for fans, door and frame heaters and variable switches for compartment fans.

Additional insulation was also installed on the doors and door frames. The typical temperature reached in Smith's evaluations was below -40° C (Smith 1984, 1986). A number of institutions in the U.S. and Canada have purchased these freezers for use in disinfesting collections and as a preventive measure for incoming acquisitions. (Smith 1985; Wei T'o® Associates 1984, 1988)

Other institutions report the use of manual-defrost and frost-free commercial and household freezers, both chest and upright models. Household freezers are less expensive and generally have, depending on the unit, the capability to achieve and hold approximately -18° C to -30° C. Some institutions report modifications of these units so that lower temperatures can be achieved and maintained. Upright models are generally available in capacities from 5 - 20 cubic feet, and chest models from 5 - 27 cubic feet. The choice of an upright or chest model depends on budget, the type of material being frozen and the floor space available. In general, books appear to be more suitable for treatment in an upright model - ease of loading and provision of air circulation. On the other hand, chest freezers tend to be more energy efficient (temperature loss is less when opened) and are generally lower in cost.

Commercial freezers are more expensive and have, depending on the unit, the capability to achieve and hold -30° C to -42° C. The majority of these freezers are upright models and capacity ranges from approximately 25-50 cubic feet.

Florian (1990{a}) recommends not to use a frost-free freezer, as they do not maintain a steady low temperature, but regularly warm up/cool down to clear frost formation. The advantages of the frost-free feature are that it keeps the unit clean, requires no manual defrosting and slows down the cooling process, thereby creating less condensation. Frost-free household freezers are difficult to find.

It is preferable that the freezer have a fan to provide air circulation, to accelerate the cooling rate and minimize condensation. Household freezers generally do not have fans, although frost-free upright models with fans are available. Recording of the internal temperature of the freezer is critical, as well as cooling rate, time at minimum temperature and thawing rate. This can be achieved in various ways, i.e. thermocouples, thermistor probes, etc.

6.2.4.3 Staff/Operator

All reports regarding staff/operator requirements indicate that library personnel trained in the use and operation of a freezer for this application poses no problems. Yale notes that a crew of two to three people with a supervisor undertook their complete operation (37,000 books). Physical plant personnel may assist with operations and maintenance.

6.2.4.4 Temperature/Relative Humidity/Time/Other

Review of the literature indicates some variation with regard to treatment parameters, both time and temperature:

■ Florian provides the most extensive review and discussion of the mechanisms and effects of freezing for cultural institutions (1986, 1990{a}). She recommends the following:

- That when using a chest freezer and the artifact is large (i.e. furniture) pre-treated silica gel or other absorbent materials can be used to maintain a relative humidity in the freezer below 100%.
- That items sealed (see 6.2.4.5 Pre-Treatment Procedures) but not yet treated, be maintained at room temperature above 18° C until placed in the freezer. In an emergency, they may be temporarily placed in a refrigerator (5° C) until freezer space is available. Temporary cold storage at temperatures above 5° C is not recommended. See 6.2.5.1 Effectiveness of Disinfestation.
- That there be adequate air circulation around items to allow for a cooling phase down to 0° C in 4 hours.
- That a minimum temperature of -20° C be maintained throughout an exposure phase of 48 hours.
- That a controlled and gradual recovery or thaw phase is desirable. An increase in temperature up to 0° C over 8 hours is suggested.
- That an immediate repetition of the freeze-thaw cycle is desirable.
- That the items remain sealed until room temperature is reached and there is no longer condensation on the exterior of the bags.

■ In the Yale situation, Remington (Peabody Museum of National History) who normally used a temperature of -23° C over 48 hours initially recommended freezing of the infested collections over seven days. Ultimately, the programme determined was deep freezing at -29° C for a period of 72 hours. Yale's blast freezer was able to reach and hold -29° to - 32° C within four to five hours after full loading and start up at normal room temperature of 21° C (Nesheim 1984). Remington was also reported as having done his own tests on silverfish, roaches, book lice and mites, as well as several stages of common household insect pests, and obtained 100% kill using -20° F (-29° C), over 72 hours, the temperature and time he had recommended for Yale (Florian 1986). The effectiveness of this treatment has recently been confirmed by Tom Strang at the Canadian Conservation Institute (Postlethwaite 1991).

■ Results of recent experimental trials for *Stegobium paniceum* (Linneaus), the drugstore beetle, showed 100% mortality for all developmental stages at -20° C, 75-85% RH, after 2 hours. It was acknowledged that under practical working conditions (insulated insects in collections vs unprotected insects) longer exposure periods may be required as various forms of freeze-resistance might occur. It was concluded that the observed results for *Stegobium paniceum* support the provisional treatment schedule proposed by Florian (1986). (Gilberg and Brokerhof 1991)

■ Smith reports that the freeze treatment in which books are brought below -29° C within 12 hours and below -40° C within 24 hours from start-up time for a minimum of 24 hours will kill the eggs, larvae, pupae and adult stages of insect life. No studies are available for the -40° C temperature. (Smith 1984)

- The Law Library of the University of California, Berkeley followed Yale's example of 72 hours at -20° F (-29° C). The freezing was undertaken at a commercial blast freezing facility. Thermocouples were not used, rather, the library relied on the company's assurance that the facility could meet these requirements.

- The Humanities Research Centre at the University of Texas also treated, at an external blast freezing facility, an infested collection at -30° F (-35.5° C). Temperature in the freezer was unable to be monitored internally - the freezer was set at -30° F for 72 hours. And, in 1989, the Metropolitan Toronto Reference Library treated a cockroach infestation of 560 books by deep-freezing at an external facility. Treatment was undertaken at -40° C for 24 hours. Monitoring was undertaken for a year and the operation was considered successful.

- Experiences in institutions in North America using the Wei T'o® Book Dryer - Insect Exterminator indicate temperatures of -29° C for a minimum of 72 hours. These include Columbia University, the Maine State Archives, the Newberry Library, and the National Archives of Canada. Infestations of book lice and various beetles were considered to have been effectively treated. (Brown-Gort 1991; Clark 1991; Tenhoor 1991; Holmes 1990; Smith 1990)

- Ketcham (1984) investigated freezing on *Dermestes maculatus* Degeer, the hide beetle. Her experimental results demonstrated a time/temperature relationship, and that all stages of the hide beetle life cycle could be killed at exposures of -12° C for 48 hours, - 15° C for 24 hours and -20° C or -23° C for 4 hours.

- Pinniger (1989) states that temperatures of -18° C or lower will kill insects if maintained for at least 7 days. He notes that this can be achieved by conventional freezing techniques or freeze-drying.

In summary, the most commonly reported temperature/time formula for libraries is -29° C for 72 hours. A variety of species of insects at various life stages were reported to have been successfully eradicated by this treatment. It is not known whether or not higher temperatures would have accomplished similar effects. However, it should be noted that treatment in a household freezer at -20° C for 48 hours has also apparently been used with success.

6.2.4.5 Pre-Treatment Procedures

It is assumed that prior to actual pre-treatment freezing procedures, investigation of the infestation would have been carried out including identification of the species of insect and life stage where possible, determination of treatment priorities, extent/location of infestation, source of infestation, etc.

No preselection treatment of library materials has been identified as being necessary in the literature.

Bagging and sealing of items is not necessary in a specially-designed controlled temperature/relative humidity freezer. This is because air is continually circulated to maintain a temperature and relative humidity balance as the items are warmed to room temperature. In other freezers (most commercial and household units) bagging and sealing of materials is necessary to prevent dramatic moisture content changes, as well as the formation of condensation on the cold books when removed from the freezer. Bagging of materials upon discovery of an infestation may also serve to limit its spread and can be used as a post-treatment isolation measure for monitoring effectiveness of the process.

Yale's procedure for the bagging of items has been modified. Initially, items were individually bagged in clear polyethylene using a specially-designed sealing machine. With two staff approximately one hundred books per hour could be bagged. Yale now boxes items and bags the entire box. Other institutions reported the use of tape, twist ties and zip-lock bags. Complete sealing permits materials to buffer the environment in the bag and protects them from moisture gain during defrost cycles, upon removal from the freezer and in the event of equipment failure. Air should be partially evacuated, the amount depending on the configuration and fragility of the item. It has been noted that precautions need to be taken. As soon as an infested item is bagged, the insects will respond to the environmental change and try to escape; therefore, immediate sealing is critical (Florian 1986). Plastic bags also vary in their ability to be penetrated by insects (see 7.4 Insect-Resistant Containers and Packaging).

The University of California Law Library, Berkeley, packed their books, spine down, in polyethylene bags in acid-free record storage boxes bottom-lined with bubble wrap. Excess air was removed, the bag closed and secured with a plastic tie. Movement during transit was minimized with additional bubble wrap. The boxes were then palletized and shrink-wrapped. Staff time for packing was minimized due to the fact that, being uncatalogued, order of the books was not critical. (Boal 1990)

The Metropolitan Toronto Reference Library packed their books in polyethylene bags (zip-lock and tape sealed) in stackable plastic storage boxes. Larger books were bagged individually and smaller items were packed together in bags. Air was manually evacuated. As with the Berkeley situation, movement in transit was minimized with bubble wrap, and as the books were uncatalogued staff time was lessened somewhat. This time saving was more than offset by that taken to bag the 560 items. It is planned that the practice of individual bagging not be repeated and that a single large bag for each box be used in the future. As part of the process, all boxes in which the infested materials had arrived were discarded immediately.

As previously noted, it is recommended that bagged materials should be kept at room temperature (above 18° C) until being placed in the freezer. It would be useful to include in the freezer load, a sampling of live insects in a glass vial where possible.

Stewart (1988) reported the need for dehumidification (prior to freezing) of an infested book collection, in an environmental chamber as previous humidity storage conditions were assumed to be high. There was concern that a high moisture content could cause swelling and disfigurement. The moisture content of the books ranged between 8 and 9% after dehumidification.

Smith (1984) states the arrangements of books in the blast freezer is not a critical factor. Books may be placed flat or standing up; however, it is suggested that they be arranged in groups with one inch spacing for the purpose of aiding air circulation. In his investigations, the stacks of books did not exceed 12 inches and the rows did not exceed 30 inches in length. He proposes that the rate of cooling may be accelerated by the insertion of aluminum foil every hundred pages in books. This would likely be too disruptive for many disinfestation operations.

6.2.4.6 Post-Treatment Procedures

Bagged items should remain bagged and sealed until all condensation is gone from the exterior of the bags and the item has reached room temperature. Recovery of the frozen materials to room temperature in the case of the temperature and RH controlled freezer such as the Wei T'o® Book Dryer-Insect Exterminator takes place in the freezer. A defrost cycle is initiated, following which the compressor and defrost components are turned off and all freezer heat sources, evaporator fan, compartment fans, fluorescent lights, and door and door frame heater are turned on. It is noted that the heat sources, except for the compact fans, should function only when the freezer can be checked once an hour for overheating. The materials may be removed once the centres of large books have reached temperatures above the dew point, about $10°$ C. (Smith 1986)

In the case of other freezers, the temperature of the freezer can be slowly increased up to $0°$ C over a period of 8 hours or so. Alternatively, where the rate of increase of temperature cannot be controlled, materials should be moved directly into a refrigerator or other cold storage until thawed. A slow rate of thawing is desirable (Florian 1986, 1990).

In order to ensure efficacy of the treatment, it is advisable to leave the items bagged for a period of time, the length of which depends on the insect species and stage of development. As freezing delays their development, maximum times should be used. Yale's materials remained bagged for six to eight months until inspection of the bait-traps in the affected areas yielded no sign of any infestation. Even previously frozen materials required for reader's use were rebagged until the project was declared complete. Items not bagged should also be quarantined. Once efficacy of the treatment is assured, materials should be cleaned of all insect remains where present.

Determination of mortality following the freezing (or other processes) should be a straightforward process, moreso, if the treatment parameters are well established. Insects, other than those in the egg stage usually demonstrate response to light or show signs of movement. If an insect is freeze-resistant it should, upon thawing, resume its normal stimulation responses or if in a state of dormancy, it will retain its original colour and hardness. If dead, an insect should show some signs of decomposition (softening, loss of colour and form) in a few days. The egg stage may be cultured; however, with experience, it should be possible to identify recognizable mortality characteristics (eggs will shrivel, harden and change in colour). (Stewart 1983)

Documentation of all procedures should be undertaken and retained. The record should include: the date of the infestation; identification, stages and activity of the insects; damages caused; bagging materials and method; temperature, relative humidity and time for cool down, exposure and recovery; and changes observed in the materials as a result of freezing. While it may be difficult and time-consuming to document all of the findings, activities and procedures, such information in many cases proves to be invaluable.

6.2.5   RESULTS

6.2.5.1 Effectiveness of Disinfestation

Insects are poikilotherms, that is their body temperature follows closely that of the surrounding environment. Thus, in general, the insect's activity and metabolic rate decreases as its body temperature is lowered until it shows no activity. A further decrease in temperature will result in death. This thermal death point varies with each insect species and is time and temperature dependent. Thus, the time at the minimum temperature of the freezing process is critical. While the actual causes of injury and death in insects are not yet fully understood, both chemical and mechanical changes and disruptions may occur.

In general, insect species that do not normally experience low temperatures in their native habitat are less tolerant of the cold, and more susceptible to injury and death by freezing. This would include most household, stored-product and museum or library pests. Cases have, however, been reported of household/museum pests surviving freezing temperatures.

With reference to the effects of freezing, insects can be categorized as follows:

- Freeze-sensitive insects that are killed at above freezing temperatures;
- Freeze-sensitive insects that are killed as soon as their tissue freezes, at around $0°$ C;
- Freeze-tolerant insects that can survive the freezing of cells and tissues (only a few species exist and have adapted to life in arctic conditions);
- Freeze-resistant insects that can withstand freezing by the demonstration of various avoidance mechanisms including cold-acclimation, prevention of ice nucleation, dehydration, and supercooling.
(Florian 1986; Mullen and Arbogast 1984; Wigglesworth 1972)

Clearly, insect freeze-resistance is a critical issue, although it is reported that there is no research available that definitely proves that household or museum insect pests can or cannot become freeze-resistant. There are suggestions that they do not. Until such time as conclusive evidence is available, it is necessary to use procedures that do not mimic those that naturally cause/encourage freeze-resistance (Florian 1986, 1990{a}).

Freeze-resistance occurs in insects on exposure to gradually falling temperatures. Cold acclimation and supercooling ability (the insect remains unfrozen below its freezing point) are the two most critical physiological states to guard against. Cold acclimation can occur if infested material is exposed to a cool environment before freezing or if the temperature lowering rate during freezing is too slow (Florian 1990{a}). The factors which influence supercooling are still uncertain; however, it is reported that repeated freezing and thawing eliminates supercooling and freezing occurs as soon as the freezing point is reached (Wigglesworth 1972).

It is reported that the acclimation (cold) process occurs in 4 - 18 hours, as long as the insect is at a temperature at which it can still move - inactive insects cannot acclimate. Insects can also undergo heat acclimation, with the result that their tolerance to low temperatures is substantially reduced if they are situated in unusually warm temperatures (Wigglesworth 1972). The temperature at which the activity of an insect ceases, and though alive is unable to acclimate, is called the chill-coma temperature. This temperature has not been established for household or museum pests, 5° C should be used as a safe margin (Florian 1986).

To make the insects most susceptible to freezing they should be acclimated at room temperature (18° C) before freezing, and then cooled in the freezer to approximately 5° C in at least four hours. This rate of cooling in the freezing process should be rapid enough to bring the insects below their chill-coma temperature and vulnerable to the exposure to -20° C temperature over 48 hours. (Florian 1986, 1990{a})

Other factors can affect insect's susceptibility to cold temperatures. While there is insufficient information to conclude that the different life stages vary in degree of freeze-resistance, it is reported that the non-feeding stages of insects are more freeze-resistant.

Information in the literature on the rate of cooling of materials in freezers indicates a slow rate of cooling for densely packed materials (Mullen and Arbogast 1979). Florian (1986) indicates that while limited data is available in this area, this research suggests the need for shelving to isolate materials and the need for temperature monitoring equipment. It further suggests that the freezer load should be kept to a reasonable minimum (balance the cooling rate and number of items to be treated) and that air circulation is important.

Florian concludes that:

> To be lethal to insects, the freezing procedure should result in cellular damage from dehydration effects, intracellular ice formation, the loss of bound water, or the reduction of enzyme activity. Supercooling should not be allowed to occur during the freezing procedure. The rate of freezing and thawing must allow cell damage to occur. The minimum temperature must be below the supercooling limit. The time held at freezing temperatures must be sufficient to allow intracellular ice crystal growth. Thus, flash freezing and thawing must be avoided. If possible, specimens should be thawed slowly in a refrigerator. (Florian 1990{a}, 4)

In summary, the freezing process should be controlled to render insects most vulnerable to the action of freezing, and to prevent freeze-resistance. The lethal effects of freezing are determined by a number of factors: the temperature/time of the insects prior to exposure to low temperature; the lowest temperature achieved and the length of time at which that temperature is maintained; the rate of freezing and thawing; the species of insect and its life stage; the nature/format/volume of the infested materials; and the manner in which they are wrapped and placed in the freezer.

The growth and metabolic activity of bacteria, yeasts and fungi are reduced at $0°$ C, but death does not occur. It is reported that $-20°$ C is lethal to the vegetative stage of certain fungi (Barton 1949). Florian was reported as stating that for mould, bacteria and fungi "repeated freeze thaw cycles are most effective, because the surviving population decreases with each cycle. For the greatest exterminating effect, the temperature should reach $-40°$ C" (Swartzburg 1987). That is not to say effective extermination will result from such treatment, for spores can remain viable in subfreezing conditions.

As stated, the literature contains few fully documented cases of freezing for insect eradication in cultural institutions, fewer still for libraries. Most relevant research has been done for the food and the stored product industries.

Yale University's deep freezing procedure for eradication of *Gastrallus*, the Death-Watch beetle was $-29°$ C for 72 hours. Remington, who proposed the use of this process to the University states that this will kill all stages of domestic insects. Yale also froze other non-book materials containing cellulose, i.e. wooden book shelves and paper office supplies (Nesheim 1984). Deep-freezing tests were conducted in 1976 prior to full implementation of the programme - 10% of the treated books were examined and no live insects were found. It is reported that Remington investigated the lethal temperature of *Gastrallus* and other insects found in libraries and found exposure at $-23°$ C for 48 hours would be effective. The temperature of $-29°$ C was selected to allow for error in temperature fluctuation. (Smith 1984). More recent research undertaken by Remington at Yale, Strang at the Canadian Conservation Institute and Child at the Welsh Folk Museum confirmed that the treatment of $-30°$ C for 72 hours provides maximum assurance (Postlethwaite 1991).

The Berkeley Law Library also treated a species of *Gastrallus* at -29° C for 72 hours and considers the operation successful. Experiences in other institutions have indicated similar successes at -29° C for 72 hours, -34° C for 72 hours, as well as -40° C for 24 hours (See 6.2.2 History of Use and 6.2.4.4 Temperature/Relative Humidity/Time/Other).

Overall, the literature on insect eradication by freezing used in cultural institutions reports successful treatments. The temperature ranges reported varied from -20° C to -40° C, with the most common being -20° C or -29° C. Time varied between 24-72 hours. Only two less-than-successful cases were found - the Perth and Inverness Museums in Scotland reported that the golden spider beetle and the webbing clothes moth survived deep-freezing at -18° C for a period of 48 hours (Stansfield 1985). It may be that those species require a longer exposure time at that temperature and/or a lower exposure temperature, or that freeze resistance was created.

Mullen and Arbogast (1979) recommend that the susceptibility of the particular species and strain of insect be determined by conducting exposure tests with the eggs. The time required to kill uninsulated eggs at a given temperature would be added to the time required to chill the commodity (host material) to that temperature. Thus, the effective low temperature exposure could be identified. This is probably not feasible for any institutions.

6.2.5.2 Effects on Books and Other Materials

Deep-freezing has the potential for use on a wide variety of library collections; however, the effects on the various constituent materials are, it appears, largely unknown. And, as Florian has stated, the composite nature of books (paper, synthetic adhesives, leather, cloth) makes generalizations and recommendations on freezing difficult (Swartzburg, 1987).

Of those institutions that have employed this process, none have reported negative side effects, although it appears results have largely been evaluated on the basis of visual examination alone. Yale has the most experience, with over 14 years in the use of freezing, both as an eradication method and as a preventive measure for incoming collections.

Studies on the effect of low temperature have been undertaken in the medical and food industries, and damages caused by ice crystal formation and other changes have been identified. The effects of freezing on books, documents and other man-made artifacts have been examined only to a limited extent. Florian, however, has undertaken research in this area and has reviewed the literature and the effects of low temperature on wood, adhesives, textiles, synthetic polymers and seeds. She notes that very little pertinent information was found on changes in materials due to the freezing temperatures that would be used for insect eradication (Florian 1986). Thus available knowledge is based on practical experience, freeze-drying of waterlogged materials, experience with extreme winter conditions and materials research from other fields such as refrigeration and cryobiology.

Of principal concern are the consequences of the formation of ice crystals in the water present in the materials frozen. Slow freezing results in the formation of large crystals, while fast freezing yields many small crystals. The specific damages that may be caused to books, papers, etc. are yet to be identified. The treatment of some composite materials may be problematic, and could result in splitting, cracking and crazing. Fragile or friable materials may require special consideration.

In her 1986 and 1990 reviews, Florian summarized the effects of freezing on the physical characteristics of materials. In wood, decrease in freezing temperatures cause increase in strength characteristics, also increase in moisture content increases these strength characteristics. At low temperatures, shrinkage may occur in wood of constant moisture content, but swelling of wood will occur if increase in moisture content accompanies temperature decrease. The literature showed variable results for adhesives. Textiles do not become brittle until the temperature drops significantly below -20° C. Most plastics become stiff, but not significantly at -20° C. Seed viability may be altered by freezing.

Also of concern is the formation of condensation which occurs where the temperature is lowered and the air has lessened ability to contain water vapour. The vapour will condense when the temperature falls below the dew point. This can also be a problem when frozen materials are being thawed and warmer air contacts the cold surface of the materials. A constant RH in the freezer can reduce the risks of condensation, such as in the Wei T'o® Book Dryer-Insect Exterminator. Alternatively, materials can be bagged and remain so until the contents have thawed and reached room temperature, at which time condensation on the outside of the bags will cease.

With regard to water relationships, three factors are of concern: the freezing of the water in the material; the freezing and condensation of water vapour in the air of the freezer or bag; and the moisture relationships between the air in the bag and the regain ability of the material. Florian (1986) concludes that dehydration effects or increase in chemical reactions will not occur and ice will not form in dry artifact materials subjected to the -20° C temperature she recommends for insect eradication. She attributes this to the low moisture content of the artifact materials which would increase due to the temperature drop, but would not be sufficient for the formation of ice.

Brokerhof (1989) reports that according to Zagulyaeva, the freezing of woody paper reduces the resistance to attack by fungi over time, and that the effect is less distinct for rag paper.

6.2.5.3 Safety and Effect on Personnel

Deep-freezing treatment is a straightforward procedure and the hazards involved are limited to that of moving/lifting items and handling cold materials. No chemicals are introduced. Thus, there is no effect direct or indirect on human health and safety, or that of the environment.

6.2.5.4 Effect on Library Operations

The impact on library operations depends upon a number of factors, principally the extent of the infestation, whether or not materials will be treated in-house or off-site and the capacity and capabilities of the freezer. The necessity for bagging will also substantially effect the rate and complexity of the operation. Documentation, retrieval, transport and reshelving of materials are also important considerations.

The number/volume of materials that can be treated depends upon the available internal "working" space of the freezer. A blast freezer of the supermarket type with 40 cubic feet of interior space is estimated to be capable of treating four to six hundred books at a time in a three day cycle (Smith 1988).

Yale University uses a 10' x 11' x 8' walk-in blast freezer. In 1977 each item was individually bagged in polyethylene and packed on carts which were then rolled into the freezer. 37,000 books plus an unidentified number of non-book and other materials were treated in 115 loads. As noted, the process has now been adapted such that items are just boxed and then each box is bagged.

6.2.6 COSTS

The total cost of deep-freezing treatment can vary considerably depending on a number of factors:

- Cost of purchase or construction of an in-house freezer/facility and attendant operating and maintenance costs.
- Cost of purchase of services of an external freezing operation including transportation and insurance.
- Cost of supplies including bags, boxes, etc.
- Cost of staff time to retrieve, prepare, treat, clean, reshelve and monitor collections, as well as documentation.

The following costs are based on information available in the literature and discussions with various institutions and vendors.

The cost of an in-house freezer or facility is as follows:

Estimated
[Note: $1 Canadian (CDN.) equals approximately $0.85 U.S.]   1991 $CDN.

- Household freezer (manual defrost) with a capacity of approximately 20 cubic feet and ability to achieve and hold -18° C to -32° C. Price range depends on specifications, i.e. chest versus upright.   750-1,250

	Estimated 1991 $CDN.

- Household freezer (frost-free) with a capacity of approximately 17 cubic feet and ability to achieve and hold - 18° C to -32° C. Price range depends on specifications, i.e. chest versus upright. — 950-1,500

- Industrial freezer (frost-free) with a capacity of approximately 25 cubic feet and ability to achieve and hold -32° C. No air circulation or monitoring equipment. — 3,000

- Industrial freezer (frost-free) with a capacity of approximately 50 cubic feet and ability to achieve and hold -30° C with forced air circulation. Includes 7-day temperature recorder. — 5,000

- Wei T'o® Book Dryer - Insect Exterminator with capacity of approximately 40 cubic feet and ability to achieve and hold -40° C. Temperature and humidity controlled. Price range depends on specifications. Commercial freezer specifically adapted for purposes of book drying and insect extermination. Price in Canada. — 21,500-25,000

- Blast freezer room with capacity of approximately 750 cubic feet and ability to achieve and hold -40° C. Temperature and humidity controlled. Price range depends on specifications. — 18,000-30,000

The cost of services of an external facility is as follows:

- Berkeley Law Library reported costs for two loads of books: 65 boxes of 1300 books and 18 boxes of 360 books. Charges were based on $3.00 U.S. per hundred weight with a minimum charge of $50.00 U.S. (Boal 1990). — 150

The cost of bags is as follows:

- Polyethylene. Price depends upon thickness of film, size of bag (5" x 7" - 36" x 36"), zip-lock feature and size of order. — 20-120 per 100

The Royal British Columbia Museum reported a cost of $40,000 for the total operation of examination, freezing, packing etc., for an unspecified number of 10,000 items (bedding, books, games, letters, etc.) infested with the case-making clothes moth (Wilson 1990).

6.2.7 BENEFITS AND RISKS

The benefits and risks of deep-freezing treatment are summarized as follows:

- **Considerable development/advancement of technology for library application.**
  Experience with library collections goes back over 14 years. Many successes have been reported.

- **Toxic chemical problems are eliminated.**
  Freezing avoids the problems of toxic chemical use, storage and disposal. No chemical residues/by-products in collections.

- **Negligible hazards to human health and safety.**
  Operation and maintenance of equipment does not pose any significant risks. No hazard to users of treated materials.

- **Operation of facility/equipment does not require certification, registration, etc.**
  The application of deep-freezing for the purpose of disinfestation is not covered by legislation.

- **Effective disinfestation of insects.**
  Treatment appears to be effective in killing all stages of insect species that may infest library collections. There remains some variation as to recommended treatment parameters.

- **Retardation of growth and activity of fungi.**
  Freezing is not considered an effective disinfestation method for fungi.

- **Post-treatment residual protection against reinfestation.**
  None is provided. Collections must be returned to conditions of good storage.

- **To date, no identified detrimental effects on library collections.**
  It appears that books, documents etc., may be treated without damage. Care must be exercised regarding condensation during the recovery phase. Identification of the effects is incomplete.

- **Application to variety of library materials.**
  It appears that many different types of collections (sizes, materials and format) may be safely and effectively treated. The treatment of fragile or friable materials or those of a complex, composite nature could be problematic.

- **Effective use as a preventive measure.**
  Freezing can be and is used as a preventive treatment for incoming collections.

- **Widely available process.**
  Freezing can be undertaken in-house, on a co-operative basis, as well as externally by commercial operations. It is flexible in its application and can be modified to suit specific requirements.

- **Application by library staff.**
  Equipment is familiar to staff. Highly specialized and extensive training is unnecessary.

- **Minimal pre- and post-treatment procedures.**
  Preparation and post-treatment activities are straight forward and minimal. Moreso with a temperature and RH controlled freezer.

- **Rapid turn-around time.**
  Materials may be treated quickly in-house and made available to users. Longer turn-around could be expected from an external treatment facility.

- **Low cost.**
  Per-item cost overall is minimal/moderate relative to other alternatives.

- **Additional functions.**
  Modified freezers can also be used to stabilize and dry water-wetted books and other materials.

6.2.8   FURTHER RESEARCH

While freezing appears to offer a fully safe, effective and affordable alternative to chemical treatment, research is required in a number of areas so that optimum treatment parameters may be determined. These include:

- The effects of freezing on the constituent materials of library collections.

- The efficacy and effects of low temperature shock.

- The penetration of low temperatures in closely packed materials.

- The effects and efficacy of freezing on life stages of various insect species.

- The freeze resistant capabilities of library infesting insects.

- The effect of repeated treatments on insects.

- The effects and efficacy of freezing on developmental stages of various fungi.

Note: A co-operative research project on the effects and effectiveness of various alternatives to EtO fumigation has been proposed. The investigation would include freezing, as well as ionizing radiation, controlled atmospheres and biological control methods. (Brokerhof 1989)

6.3   HIGH-ENERGY IRRADIATION: GAMMA

6.3.1   DESCRIPTION

Both insects and fungi can be killed with high-energy radiation, although fungi are more difficult to eradicate. The lethal effect of radiation in living cells is caused by changes in enzymes and other substances essential to life processes. Two types of high-energy radiation can be applied: electromagnetic radiation and charged particles with high energy. Three types of high-energy electromagnetic radiation exist: gamma, röntgen and far ultraviolet radiation.

To date, gamma radiation has been the only method reported for use in disinfestation of library, herbarium and museum collections.   Studies have been undertaken regarding the effects of röntgen and far ultraviolet radiation; both of which have an insecticidal, and possibly a fungicidal effect. Charged particles with high energy, or beta radiation is a direct source of high-energy electrons and its mechanism of effects on organisms and materials is the same as for gamma radiation. Studies on the effects of beta radiation have been undertaken on cellulose, paper, cotton, hides and leathers, and synthetic materials (Brokerhof 1989).

Chappas and McCall (1986) identify the practical sources of radiation as Cobalt-60 gamma rays and electrons from accelerators, for reasons of price, availability and penetration. Neither of these two sources induce radioactivity in the material being treated and there are no restrictions on the subsequent handling of material, irrespective of the applied dose. In their opinion, disinfestation of collection materials will be limited largely to contract Cobalt-60 irradiators. The advantages over electron sources are that they are widely distributed and commercially accessible, they provide penetration power for complete disinfestation of large boxes and the price is competitive with other techniques.

The mechanism of the effects of high-speed electron (beta) and gamma radiation on organisms and materials is the same. Gamma radiation is produced by the nuclear disintegration of radioactive isotopes (Cobalt-60). Electrons are generated within the materials when radiation is absorbed. Beta radiation is a direct source of high-energy electrons and is produced by the emission of these electrons from a heated cathode beamed across an electron scan. Beta radiation can only be used for the treatment of material exposed in thin layers up to about 1.7 cm depending on the energy output of the accelerator (Watters 1984). Moisture can further limit penetration.

6.3.2   HISTORY OF USE

Gamma radiation is currently used to sterilize and control microorganisms in cosmetics, food and agriculture products and packaging, medical supplies, as well as hospital and laboratory equipment.   It is also routinely used in manufacturing processes where absorption of radiation is used to modify materials to economic advantage, such as the curing of coatings and polymer modification. Industry opinion is that radiation processing will become more widespread. This is largely due to the fact that it is becoming economically competitive with other conventional technologies where costs for energy, labour and modifications required by chemical regulation are increasing. Gamma radiation is much more widely used in Europe. In 1985, there were about 20 large scale gamma radiation facilities in the United States, with several under construction (Story 1985). In 1986, more than 500 radiation processing facilities were reported as operational throughout the world (Chappas and McCall 1986).

Gamma radiation has been used on a small but significant scale in a number of countries for the purpose of disinfestation of museum, library and archival collections. The literature revealed considerable research on the effects of radiation; however, there were found few documented cases of the use of this method in cultural institutions, particularly libraries.

In 1982, the Alan Mason Chesney Medical Archives of the Johns Hopkins Medical Institutions conducted a pilot project in the use of gamma radiation to disinfest a large collection of historic manuscripts. The Archives had been willed the collection which was housed in a dilapidated building in Baltimore. The collection was large, approximately 300 cubic feet and was extensively infested by insects, rodents, cats, dogs, and various species of fungi, and was covered in dust and soot. There were also desiccated animal specimens, as well as unidentified chemicals and drugs. Intellectual value, as opposed to artifactual value of the papers was considered to be of paramount importance. The collection was treated at a commercial radiation facility, and was considered successful for this application. No damage from radiation has been noted to date, although results are considered incomplete. (McCall 1985, 1990)

Since 1982, the Museum of Central Bohemia at Roztoky has operated a conservation irradiation facility (using Cobalt-60) for the purpose of centralized treatment of objects from art and museum collections. The collections include wooden objects, as well as those made of paper, textiles, leather, wicker and straw. The radiation disinfestation method was studied extensively and a radiation and chemical treatment procedure developed. Radiation is considered successful for the eradication of both insects and fungi. Because radiation does not provide protection against future attack, it was considered necessary (in 1978) to further treat certain wood objects with a surface coating containing an insecticide. (Urban et al. 1978; Urban and Justa 1986). Research has further been undertaken at this preservation radiation centre on gamma radiation as a means of disinfesting books and documents. Similar work has also been reported in Romania (Hanus 1985). Gamma radiation was also noted for use for the petrification of damaged wood objects impregnated with a resin-monomer system. This process, developed in France, is applicable to dry and waterlogged wood, as well as stone (Urban et al. 1978).

Gamma radiation research into the disinfestation of library and archival materials has also been reported in China. Experiments were carried out at the Sichuan Province Institute of Nuclear Technology Application where two types of treatment were undertaken, 'lump' radiation and 'transport' radiation. Subsequently, over one million volumes were reported to be treated with good results. (Chengfa et al. 1988)

Ionizing radiation was used to ensure eradication of fungi on the mummy of Ramses II. Pre-treatment testing of the 18 kGy dose to be applied was undertaken on the constituent materials (Ramière 1981).

Gamma radiation is also a component of the British Library graft polymerization process. Books are coated with monomers, then irradiated which changes the monomers to polymers which strengthen the paper while protecting against further acidification.

6.3.3 PROCESS

In summary, the radiation process consists of four stages:

1. Pre-treatment procedures.
      Identification and documentation of nature and extent of infestation.
      Quarantine of infested collection.
      Bagging, sealing and boxing of materials where applicable.

2. Transportation.
      Transportation to external facility.

3. Exposure/Extermination.
      Exposure to gamma radiation.

4. Transportation.
      Return from external facility.

5. Post-treatment procedures.
      Remove materials to quarantine area.
      Determine effectiveness of treatment (live insects or new emergence).
      Examine and assess condition of materials.
      Remove insect remains, debris, etc.
      Transport materials back to conditions of good storage.
      Complete documentation record.
      Adapt process where necessary.

This process would generally only be undertaken by an external commercial facility. Gamma radiation involves radioactive materials and requires a specialized facility with appropriate shielding and monitoring apparatus, as well as highly skilled operators. However, the Museum of Central Bohemia at Roztoky in co-operation with the Nuclear Research Institute at Řež recently constructed (1976-1980) a conservation radiation facility in the museum. It is noted that it is probably the only facility of its kind in the world (Urban and Justa 1986).

6.3.4   REQUIREMENTS

6.3.4.1 Legislation

Due to the hazards involved, radiation processing in all countries is controlled by government legislation.

6.3.4.2 Equipment/Facility

As noted, the treatment of books and paper materials would in most cases be undertaken by contract Cobalt-60 irradiators. These facilities are widely distributed and commercially accessible. Such facilities use a planar rack of Cobalt-60 rods, doubly encapsulated in stainless steel that is raised out of a water storage well for use. The boxes to be treated are moved past the radiation source by means of a conveyer system. (Chappas and McCall 1986)

The Museum of Central Bohemia radiation facility is located in the basement of the former brewery of a 17th century castle. It consists of five rooms (radiation chamber, operators' room, store-room, manipulation room and conservation laboratory) with a total area of 120 m². The dimensions of the radiation chamber are 4.5 x 4.5 x 3.6 m. The shielding power of the original 1 m thick walls was increased, the ceiling rebuilt, and other necessary modifications made. The Cobalt-60 source is located under the floor of the chamber in a lead and steel container, which is brought into irradiating position with a shielding plug. Extensive electrical and mechanical blocking, signalling, monitoring and emergency systems were installed to ensure the safety of the operations staff.

6.3.4.3 Staff/Operator

As gamma radiation is produced by the nuclear disintegration of radioactive isotopes, highly specialized staff are required to undertake the operation of a radiation facility.

6.3.4.4 Temperature/Relative Humidity/Time/Other

Research has been undertaken in many disciplines to study the effectiveness and effects of radiation. The literature indicates that there remain a variety of opinions as to the minimum lethal dose for various organisms. The biological effect depends on the absorbed dose, the dose rate, irradiated medium and type and age of organisms. In general, the lower organisms are more resistant to radiation than higher organisms (Brokerkof 1989).

According to Wolf, the lethal dose for insects is about 1 kGy and they become sterile at about 0.1 kGy (Brokerhof 1989). It is reported that woodworm in all stages of their life cycle can be killed at 0.25 kGy - 0.5 kGy and that the lethal dose for moths is 1 kGy - 3 kGy. (Urban and Justa 1986; Wolf 1986) Ramière noted that the dose generally used for the disinfestation of wood objects was 0.5 kGy (Ramière 1981).

Ley, in his report of the commercial status of various radiation processes, indicates 2 kGy - 50 kGy for the disinfestation and disinfection of works of art and historical objects in small scale commercial operations in France and the United Kingdom (Ley 1988).

Fungi are more resistant to radiation. Studies differ in their determination of the required lethal dose - from 4.5 kGy to 18 kGy. The Johns Hopkins pilot project achieved good results (fungi and insects) using 4.5 kGy for approximately 48 minutes. A minimum dose of 8 kGy was determined by Horakova and Martinek (1984) to be the lethal dose for mildews tested. Hanus also states an estimated dose of 8 kGy is effective for mould sterilization (Hanus 1984). Pavon Flores (1975-76) identified 18 kGy as that required to kill the fungal species she studied. She further concluded that the rate (kGy per hour) at which the dose was administered was unimportant. Research in central Czechoslovakia and Romania indicate a minimum effective dose of 6 kGy - 8 kGy depending on the species and strain. Belyakova (1960) concluded that the minimal dose for disinfestation of books was 6.5 kGy. A Quebec feasibility study on the sterilization of books and documents by gamma radiation concluded that the insects and fungi which infest library collections could be eradicated by gamma radiation with doses of 4.5 kGy - 10 kGy (Gagnon and Beaulieu 1985). Bonetti et al. (1979) reported that the growth of fungi was inhibited at 7 kGy and that a dose of 10 kGy was required to effect treatment for a range of species. 10 kGy was considered to be a relatively low dose.

An increase in temperature has a synergistic effect on the lethal effect of radiation. That is, higher temperatures can decrease the minimum effective dose required. This is critical where the doses required to eradicate the insects and fungi could damage the collections being treated. Urban (Hanus 1985) determined that a dose of 6 kGy was effective in killing four moulds tested. By raising the temperature to 60° C it became possible to reduce the minimum effective radiation dose to 0.5 kGy. The Preservation Radiation Centre in Roztoky, reports an experimental programme in the evaluation of the synergistic effect of radiation with temperatures up to 49° C with the goal of decreasing the minimum effective radioactive dose to below 0.8 kGy (Hanus 1985). A decrease in temperature necessitates a higher dose for the activity of the organisms is reduced and thus would be less sensitive.

A raised oxygen concentration in the air has a positive effect on the dose and low relative humidity results in a decreased effectiveness. Brokerhof (1989) notes that the literature provides no definite answers on the dose-rate effect. High dose-rates appear to have a better effectiveness on eradication of microorganisms. In a contract Cobalt-60 irradiator total dose is controlled by the speed of the conveyor system. A typical dose rate is 5 kGy/hour and a typical maximum dose rate is 20 kGy/hour. Low level disinfestation through to complete sterilization processing times range from 1 to 5 hours respectively. In the case of the Johns Hopkins pilot project, the radiation facility provided a quality assurance certificate detailing dosage and exposure time. Overall, absorbed dose, dose-rate, temperature and relative humidity are among the factors that affect the effectiveness of disinfestation by radiation.

Gamma radiation does produce changes in materials, many of them damaging. There is no general agreement on the dose level at which such changes occur (see 6.3.5.2 Effect on Books and Other Materials).

6.3.4.5 Pre-treatment Procedures

Based on some of the research done to date, pre-treatment selection may be necessary due to the effects of radiation on certain materials and the impact of repeated exposures (see 6.3.5.2 Effect on Books and Other Materials).

As most radiation treatments would be undertaken by an external facility, consultation would be required to ensure that the established requirements could be met. As the dose required appears to depend upon the species of fungi or insect, expertise should be sought to confirm the identity of the infestation. Arrangements must also be made for transportation of the materials to and from the radiation facility.

In the case of the Johns Hopkins project, where the infestations were extensive, an industrial hygienist reviewed the findings of a microbiologist and drew up a series of safety procedures for the packing crew. Protective gear including coveralls, particle masks, surgical caps and shoe coverings, goggles and heavy gloves were worn. It was noted that a commercial moving company refused the packing job, as being too hazardous a process. (McCall 1985)

There is little in the literature regarding the need for and the mechanics of pre-treatment preparation. Mention is made of packing books and papers in cardboard record storage boxes. The Johns Hopkins materials were dusted before being placed in boxes which were lined with heavy plastic garbage bags. When filled, the bags were twist-tied and the lids fixed, to minimize contamination hazards in transit.

6.3.4.6 Post-Treatment Procedures

The Johns Hopkins pilot project reports provide information on the procedures undertaken following return of the materials from the radiation facility. Bagged materials that had been stored in three different areas of the infested building were unsealed and a microbiologist took ten swabs. When cultured, they showed only a trace of *Penicillin* which was believed to have been introduced in the packing process.

A paper conservator undertook a thorough physical examination of eradicated samples and could not detect any obvious changes. (McCall 1985)

The effectiveness of the treatment should be determined and monitored. Materials should be kept in quarantine until disinfestation is complete and then returned to an environment appropriate to the storage of collections. Materials should also be cleaned of fungi and insect remains, and examined as to the effect of the radiation. Documentation of all aspects of the treatment should be undertaken.

6.3.5   RESULTS

6.3.5.1   Effectiveness of Disinfestation

There is no doubt that gamma radiation can be effective in killing insects, fungi and bacteria depending on a variety of factors including the dose, dose rate, temperature and relative humidity, as well as the nature of the irradiated material and the type of nature of organisms.

Insects, fungi and bacteria behave differently when exposed to radiation. The life stages of insects vary in their sensitivity to radiation. Eggs are the most vulnerable, particularly those in the latter stages of development. Irradiation of larvae can cause death, again depending on the stage of development. The effects (during and after) of radiation on pupae are varied: death, growth abnormalities, sterility and a shortened lifespan in adults. Adult insects are the most radiation resistant of the life stages although observed radiation effects include decreased/no appetite, inability to fly, etc. (Gagnon and Beaulieu 1985).

In general, spore-producing bacteria are less susceptible to radiation than those that do not produce spores. A number of mechanisms are responsible for this resistance phenomenon. The behaviour of fungi in radiation differs from that of bacteria because of differences in cytology, morphology, reproductive cycles and growth. Like bacteria, the spores are less susceptible to radiation than vegetative cells. Bacterial spores are more resistant than those of fungi (Gagnon and Beaulieu, 1985).

Extensive studies of the susceptibility of stored-product insects to various doses of ionizing radiation have been made. A characteristic feature of the process is that irradiated insects take several days or weeks to die at the doses approved for the treatment of wheat and wheat flour.

There is no current evidence to suggest that insects have become resistant to radiation. It is noted, that some insects such as cockroaches can tolerate many times more radiation than man (Boraiko 1981).

Gamma radiation has good powers of penetration which allow materials to be effectively treated in sealed containers used for transportation or storage. "Gamma radiation ... is penetrating enough to go through even the bulkiest articles with a diameter of up to 1 m .." (Urban and Justa 1986). Penetration would depend upon the energy of the radiation, the density of the material and the specific mass of the packing materials (Brokerhof 1989). Different materials and large quantities may be treated at the same time.

6.3.5.2 Effect on Books and Other Materials

A major disadvantage of radiation is the initiation of degradation processes, either immediate or over time.

Many materials, including cellulose, can degrade upon irradiation with gamma rays. As the material is radiated, the individual molecules can undergo scission sharply reducing its mechanical properties. In some instances, the final product may become so mechanically weak that the slightest stress can result in its crumbling. To complicate this phenomenon further, the number of scissions can be affected by a self-propagating reaction with oxygen. This auto-oxidative degradation may continue for days or years following the disinfestation. The oxidation process can also produce several undesirable acids in the material. Additives used in the manufacture of the product can also induce severe changes. In addition to odour problems, a yellowing of the irradiated product is often associated with additives.

All of these radiation induced degradation processes are caused by reactive free radicals in the material. Some of these free radicals are trapped in the host materials crystalline regions ... [and their] diffusion process may take months. As a result, some materials may even appear unchanged immediately following the disinfestation by radiation, only to disintegrate upon examination years later. (Chappas and McCall 1986, 371-372)

A second major disadvantage of radiation is that the effects of repeated exposures are cumulative. However, according to Urban and Justa (1986) a treatment of 0.5 kGy could be repeated up to twenty times without causing any damage to the irradiated item.

Opinions in the literature vary as to the dosage at which changes in materials are initiated, but, there is no doubt that changes do occur. The occurrence of these reactions depends on the structure of the molecules and some compounds are quite resistant to radiation. The moisture content of the materials is important, as water is sensitive to ionizing reactions. As a reduced moisture content is supposed to result in a decrease in the formation of radicals, drying or freezing of materials prior to irradiation might reduce the damage (Brokerhof 1989).

It is generally agreed that materials containing cellulose are extremely vulnerable to damaging reactions.

■ Pavon Flores (1975-76) concluded that the effects of radiation on paper vary according to its composition. The results of the measurements of the mechanical properties of the papers tested indicated no changes with doses up to circa 10 kGy. Beyond this dose, further irradiation led to marked deterioration.

- Calvini advises against the use of a 5 kGy radiation treatment based on studies of rag and chromatographic papers (The Abbey Newsletter, 1984).

- According to Urban and Justa (1986) 0.25 kGy - 0.5 kGy causes no damage to paper.

- Horakova and Martinek (1984) found that a dose of 8 kGy did not result in any particularly conspicuous changes to the papers tested. It was noted that certain reactions may take place where effects will only be seen after a longer time following treatment.

- McCall (1985) reported the use of 4.5 kGy with no observed changes to the paper materials treated.

- Hanus (1985) reported that fold endurance of all papers tested decreased with higher doses of radiation (3 kGy - 26 kGy). He concluded that an estimated dose of 8 kGy is effective for mould sterilization, but also causes degradation of treated papers.

- Butterfield (1987) found that gamma radiation resulted in a decrease of strength in the papers tested, similar to that resulting from accelerated dry aging. Radiation followed by dry aging resulted in further loss of mechanical strength. She concludes that the results obtained indicate that 10 kGy radiation causes an unacceptable level of paper degradation.

- Leclerc (1989), in her review of the results of research on the effects of gamma radiation, concluded that the lethal dose for fungi initiates unacceptable degradation in works on paper. It was reported that a dose between 0.16 and 1.6 kGy was found to be the least onerous means of killing insects.

- A recent study on the effects of radiation on bleached Kraft medical packaging papers concluded that for doses between 0 and 160 kGy, each 10 kGy increment is associated with a 3-4% reduction in paper strength. The initial losses occurring between 0 and 60 kGy tend to be greater. (Keeney and Walkinshaw 1990).

McCall notes that a dose of 4.5 kGy would not damage inks and the Smithsonian Institution's Conservation Analytical Laboratory tentatively concluded that 0.06 kGy is safe for painted media (The Abbey Newsletter 1984, 1987).

Rossi-Doria (Raimière 1981) noted a loss of adhesive strength and a hardening of animal glues at a dose of 10 kGy. According to Flieder, (Ramière 1981) leather (calf and goat) does not experience major chemical changes at a dose of 18 kGy. Chahine (Brokerhof 1989) also considered that a 18 kGy dose caused negligible degradation in leather (untanned calf skin and vegetable tanned), as well as parchment. According to Davis, and Gulik and Klopper (Brokerhof 1989) leather may soften, the tensile strength decreases as a result of irradiation and shrinkage temperature is reduced. A further reported problem associated with the radiation of paper and leather is that they become more sensitive to new microbiological attack after treatment (Brokerhof 1989).

Regarding the effect of radiation on other materials, Urban and Justa (1986) report that a dose of 0.25 kGy - 0.5 kGy does not cause damage to wood, polychrome, oil and tempera paints, surface coatings and glues, straw, textiles, leather and parchment. Doses as high as 50 to 100 times the 0.5 kGy value are reported to have no appreciable negative effect on the physico-mechanical properties of wood, nor its appearance. According to Sedlackova (Brokerhof 1989) polychromy is not damaged by radiation at doses of 0.5 kGy to 200 kGy; however, due to effects on the mechanical properties of test materials, it is concluded that a safe dose is 0.5 kGy.

Wood is, in general, considered to be less vulnerable to radiation than paper. It is believed that the presence of lignin in wood has a protective effect on the cellulose (Brokerhof 1989). Butterfield (1987) states that lignin is thought to provide cellulose some protection against radiation.

Some plastics, i.e. PVC, polypropylene, acrylics, etc. are adversely affected by radiation. Gamma radiation is also known to cause changes to cotton, including cracking of the fiber surface and loss of tensile strength (Story 1985).

6.3.5.3 Safety and Effect on Personnel

During treatment, safety is the responsibility of the commercial radiation facility. Appropriate shielding, monitoring, recording, etc., equipment and procedures that meet applicable legislation/regulation must be in place. The same applies if the process is done in-house.

Regarding the use and handling of treated materials, it appears there is no risk to human health and safety. Gamma radiation does not leave materials radioactive and there are no residues created. However, as Brokerhof (1989) points out, the chemical changes that occur in materials and the free radicals remaining could be considered as residues.

6.3.5.4 Effect on Library Operations

There is little information in the literature that discusses the impact of radiation treatment on the operation of an institution. In terms of time in a typical cobalt-60 irradiator, processing for low level disinfestation (typical coverage does rate of 5 kGy/hour) and complete sterilization (typical average dose rate of 20 kGy/hour) range from one to five hours (Chappas and McCall 1986).

Consideration must also be given to the packing of materials. In the case of the Medical Archives of the Johns Hopkins Medical Institute, eight staff packed 295 standard record centre boxes over seven working days. The materials were treated in two batches, each done in approximately 48 minutes. A total of 300 cubic feet was treated. Materials, if going offsite, must be transported and cleaned on their return. Time for examination, analysis and documentation must also be considered.

The in-house radiation facility of the Museum of Central Bohemia treats 1,850 objects of average dimension per year. The dimensions of the chamber are 4.5 x 4.5 x 3.6 m. (Urban and Justa 1986).

6.3.6 COSTS

The total cost of radiation treatment would vary considerably depending on a number of factors:

- Cost of purchase of services of an external radiation facility including transportation and insurance.

- Cost of supplies including bags, boxes, etc.

- Cost of staff time to retrieve, prepare, clean, reshelve and monitor collections, as well as documentation.

Scant information is available in the literature on costs.

- Overall budget of the Johns Hopkins project in 1983 (McCall 1985) was $2,100 U.S., the equivalent of $2,500 Canadian or $4,300 Canadian in 1991 dollars. This figure does not include the time contributed by various expert technical advisors.

Breakdown of expenses was as follows:

	Estimated
[Note: $1 Canadian (CDN.) equals approximately $0.85 U.S.]	1991 $CDN.
Protective gear for crew (due to extreme nature of infestation)	600
Ionizing radiation treatment	720
Truck rental driver cost	720
Wages for packing crew	2,060
Incidental expenses	200
Estimated cost for treatment per cubic foot	13

- It is noted that in 1985, commercial radiation facilities had an estimated construction price of $3 million U.S. (Story 1985).

- The cost for radiation treatment by a commercial facility in Quebec was estimated in 1985 to be $50 - 100 per cubic meter (Gagnon and Beaulieu 1985) or an estimated $75-150 in 1991 Canadian dollars.

6.3.7. BENEFITS AND RISKS

The benefits and risks of gamma radiation treatment are summarized as follows:

- **Minimal development/advancement of technology for library application.**
  Experience with library materials is limited compared to that for museum collections.

- **Elimination of toxic chemical problems.**
  Radiation avoids the problems of toxic chemical use, storage and disposal. No treatment chemical residues in collections. Note: Chemical changes that occur and remaining radicals could be considered residues/by-products.

- **Major hazards to human health and safety.**
  Transport, use and disposal of radioactive materials presents substantial risk. No hazard to users of treated collections - radiation does not leave materials radioactive.

- **Design, operation and maintenance of facility must meet applicable legislative/regulatory requirements.**
  Use of radioactive materials requires stringent safety restrictions.

- **Effective disinfestation of insects.**
  Treatment is reported to be effective in killing all stages of insect species that may infest library collections. There remains variation as to the recommended treatment parameters.

- **Possible effective disinfestation of fungi.**
  Fungi are reported to be difficult to eradicate.

- **Post-treatment residual protection against reinfestation.**
  None is provided. Collections must be returned to conditions of good storage.

- **Detrimental effects on library collections.**
  Damages (short- and long-term) to materials have been identified at certain dose levels. Treatment parameters are in the developmental stage.

- **Application to variety of library materials.**
  It appears that many different types of collections (size, materials and format) could be treated; however, the detrimental effects to many materials would be substantial.

- **Improbable use as a preventive measure.**
  It is unlikely that radiation would be used as a preventive measure.

- **Availability of process varied.**
  Geographic location would determine proximity/accessibility to external commercial radiation facilities. Development of in-house operation unlikely for most institutions. Limited flexibility in application.

- **Application by library staff.**
  Not applicable by regular library staff.

- **Minimal pre- and post-treatment procedures.**
  Preparation and post-treatment activities are minimal.

- **Rapid turn-around time.**
  Materials could be treated fairly quickly and made available to users. Time frame would vary depending on in-house treatment versus that done by external facility.

- **Low Cost.**
  Per-item cost for treatment by external facility is minimal relative to other alternatives.

- **Additional functions.**
  None identified to date.

6.3.8   FURTHER RESEARCH

Gamma radiation may offer an alternative to chemical treatment, particularly where collections are severely and extensively infested, although safety requirements and concerns in some countries would likely limit its use. Research is required in a number of areas so that optimum treatment parameters may be determined. These include:

- The effects of gamma radiation on the constituent materials of library collections.

- The effects and efficacy of gamma radiation on the life stages of various insect species.

- The effects and efficacy of gamma radiation on the developmental stages of various fungi.

- The effects of different conditions (i.e. temperature, moisture content) during irradiation.

- The ability of organisms to develop radiation resistance.

See Note, 6.2.8 Further Research (Deep-Freezing).

6.4   LOW-ENERGY IRRADIATION: MICROWAVE

6.4.1   DESCRIPTION

The term microwave applies generally to the higher frequency end of the radio frequency (RF) region of the electromagnetic spectrum. The RF region is situated between the audio frequencies and the infrared region. Microwaves are low-energy radiowaves, a non-ionizing form of radiation, the action of which is different from that of high-energy radiation. The energy associated with microwaves is relatively weak, almost thermal in effect.

In a microwave, electricity is converted to microwave energy by the magnetron tube. The microwaves travel from the tube to the oven cavity. Absorption of the microwaves produces heat by increasing the vibrational activity of molecules. Materials containing polar groups and sufficient moisture can absorb microwaves. The lethal effect in insects is attributed to the heat generated both in the insect's body and host material. Other non-thermal effects on insects have also been reported in the literature. These include abnormal development, prolonged pupation and shorter adult life.

Microwaves are not considered to be effective against fungi and bacteria.

Microwave radiation should not be confused with dielectric radiation. The term dielectric can be applied to a wide range of electromagnetic frequencies, while microwave radiation covers a narrower spectrum which involves shorter wavelengths.

6.4.2   HISTORY OF USE

Microwaves have, of course, been used for a number of years as a cooking tool, both for commercial and home application. Research has been done since the late 1920s on the possible use of RF energy for the control of insects. Microwave and other radiowave frequencies have been used in the food processing and agricultural industries to control insects in grains, flour, wood and other stored food products. Microwave disinfestation has also been used to a limited extent in the textile industry.

Use of microwaves in cultural institutions has largely been that of experimentation. Hall (1981) described the use of microwaves at the University of Florida Herbarium for treatment of herbarium material and the British Columbia Provincial Museum (now Royal British Columbia Museum) has also conducted experiments on specimens (Stansfield 1985). Reagan studied the control of the webbing clothes moth with microwaves (Reagan, Chiao-Cheng and Streit 1980; Reagan 1982). It was concluded that if prudently applied, microwave heating can provide a safe and effective nonchemical method of disinfesting wool textiles.

Microwaves have recently been suggested for use in the treatment of infested book materials. A paper presented by Brezner in 1988 reviewed available insect control methods for libraries, reported experimental results and recommended the use of microwave radiation. A subsequent article further described the results of what Brezner considers to be preliminary studies (Brezner 1989). Brezner indicated in discussion in March 1990 that no further work was planned.

No library or archives was found to be currently using this method for disinfestation of collections. Microwaves are, however, currently being investigated for use in the pre-drying phase of several mass deacidification processes. Also, studies by the Centre national de la recherche scientifique (CNRS) in France have been undertaken on drying of paper by a microwave dryer specially adapted for this purpose. Contrary to a standard microwave oven where the waves are disordered by a fan, single-mode wave guides were used, each supplied with a magnetron generator whose power is maintained between 0 and 800 watts. Based on the results of this work, commercialization of this dryer was reported. Its intended uses include drying after aqueous washing or deacidification, or wetting after a disaster. It was not envisioned that this dryer would be suitable for books; however, a study for this application is reported to be under way. Also planned, in collaboration with the Centre de recherches sur la conservation des documents graphiques in Paris, is research into the effectiveness of microwaves, for the purpose of disinfestation of microorganisms. A study is also reported on the modification of this dryer for the purpose of lamination. (Brandt and Berteaud 1987)

6.4.3   PROCESS

In summary, the microwave process consists of four stages:

1. Pre-treatment procedures.
    Identification and documentation of nature and extent of infestation.
    Quarantine of infested collection.
    Preselection of materials where necessary.
    Transport of materials to treatment area.
    Loading of materials in microwave.
    Placement of thermistor thermometer to remotely record temperature.

2. Exposure/Extermination.
    Materials are exposed to microwaves.
    Monitor to verify and control time/temperature equipment operation and condition/safety of material.

3. Recovery to room temperature.
    Let materials return to room temperature.

4. Post-treatment procedures.
   Remove materials to quarantine area.
   Examine and assess condition of materials.
   Determine/monitor effectiveness of treatment (live insects or new emergence).
   Remove insect remains, debris.
   Transport materials back to conditions of good storage.
   Complete documentation record.
   Adapt process where necessary.

The process described must be viewed in the context of current limited knowledge of microwave treatment of library collections. Microwave treatment is likely only to be undertaken in-house. No commercial operation is known to exist for the treatment of infested library collections.

6.4.4 REQUIREMENTS

6.4.4.1 Legislation

No legislation is known to exist regarding the disinfestation of materials by microwave radiation.

6.4.4.2 Equipment/Facility

Equipment requirements are quite modest for a basic operation - a microwave oven and temperature monitoring equipment. Basic consumer ovens (2450 MHz) are available in a number of power levels, cavity sizes and with various features.

Remote recording of book temperatures in microwaves has been done using a portable thermistor thermometer (Brezner 1988). Reagan (1982) in her disinfestation studies of wool textiles used temperature-sensitive strips. These labels contain a series of dots corresponding to various temperatures.

A more sophisticated approach for large volume treatment in a food industry application has been developed by the McDonnel Douglas Corporation where a moving belt microwave is used to control storage grain insects (Tilton and Vardell 1981). The microwave dryer developed at CNRS also employs an automated conveyor belt system, of variable speed, for the treatment of papers up to a maximum size of 50 cm. and a thickness of 5 - 6 mm (Brandt and Berteaud 1987).

6.4.4.3 Staff/Operator

Operation of a microwave oven is simple; however, staff responsible should be familiar with the types of materials, i.e. metals, that must not be placed in a microwave, and be vigilant as to the power setting and time. Radiation tests should be conducted on a routine basis.

6.4.4.4 Temperature/Relative Humidity/Time/Other

As there is very limited data available on the application of microwaves to library materials, these requirements can only be referred to in broad terms.

Clearly, internal temperature is critical as it is generally recognized that the production of heat can be problematic for many materials. Brezner directly provides no information on temperature; however, it was reported that in his experiments "the temperature of the paper in the book never exceeded 80° C, and was generally significantly below that" (DeCandido 1989). It was stated that the time for 99% kill ranged between 67.3 to 77 seconds. The lethal time to achieve 50% kill was reported as 49.6 and 53.4 seconds at medium power of 639 watts (Brezner 1988).

In Reagan's studies of wool textiles, the initial three minute period of microwave exposure resulted in temperatures of 62° - 76° C for the six monitored positions. Repeated 3 minute exposures produced similar temperature ranges. A continuous 10 minute exposure resulted in significantly higher temperature ranges of 103° - 149° C. Her recommended exposure conditions for microwave disinfestation (2450 Mz) of wool textiles are 3 minutes of continuous exposure with a minimum internal sample temperature of 69° C.

6.4.4.5 Pre-Treatment Procedures

Pre-treatment preparation/selection of library materials would be necessary, as indicated by Brezner's experiments with "a number of contemporary hardcover texts and magazines" (Brezner 1989). While he states there was no discernible change to the publications, save for some page loosening of the softcover volume, he does go on to identify precautions, some of which pertain to the use of microwaves in general and others to the treatment of library materials.

Brezner reports that his "short, moderate power [639 watts] exposures had little effect [on non-starch-based adhesives]" (Brezner 1989, 62). He states that many of the paperback editions use thermoplastic glues that may soften during irradiation and result in some loose pages. One soft-cover column did have some page loosening after microwave treatment at high power (720 watts) for 3 minutes. DeCandido (1988), in his discussion on the microwave reactivation of glue in publisher's adhesive bindings outlines a number of concerns - that animal glues may be damaged, that emulsion adhesives may be softened and that hot melts are reactivated by heat. It has also been reported that the British Columbia Provincial Museum found that the microwave affected the adhesives used in the attachment of herbarium specimens and labels (Stansfield 1985).

Brezner observed no changes "in colors, spine integrity, page appearances or print bleeding." He did note some page warping on hardcovers which ceased after fifteen minutes at normal room temperature and humidity. (Brezner 1988, 66)

Brezner states that "paper and parchment have water contents (w/w) of eight percent or less (depending on construct) and should be safe from microwave exposure" (Brezner 1989, 61). No data was provided.

Brezner (1989) and Brokerhof (1989) both identify leather as being problematic - fire damage might result as temperature inside may become very high. The same is true for other tightly packed materials. Brezner recommends that leather bindings not be microwaved and further advises that the treatment of historic volumes with older papers, pigments and bindings may be sensitive to microwave treatment.

Materials having metal inclusions or attachments should not be microwaved as sparking and incineration may result. This would include metal foil, staples, fasteners, clips, and security labels and barcodes. Instruction manuals for microwaves identify this hazard and even warn users that some recycled papers may be problematic due to metallic salts. However, many microwaves for cooking purposes allow the inclusion of small amounts of aluminum foil for shielding purposes located at least 2.5 cm from each other and the walls of the oven. Papers of a dyed or synthetic nature are not recommended for microwaving.

Microwave instruction manuals also provide warning regarding the treatment of certain plastics and recent media coverage regarding research in Britain has pointed to the possible hazardous release of chemicals from non-microwave approved food wraps and containers. This may have application to some of the plasticized and laminated papers and boards used in contemporary library materials. In addition, there may be problems with the separation of laminates on covers with a high moisture content.

6.4.4.6 Post-Treatment Procedures

No post-treatment procedures specific to microwave treatment have been identified. The effectiveness of the treatment should be determined and monitored in quarantine where necessary. When disinfestation is considered to be complete, and materials have been cleaned, they should be returned to appropriate storage conditions. Complete documentation of the process should be undertaken.

6.4.5 RESULTS

6.4.5.1 Effectiveness of Disinfestation

Microwaves have been identified as being effective for the control of a number of species of insects. Research on their lethal effects have been undertaken for a variety of grain, flour and fruit infesting insects. One study showed that the best results were obtained after a combination microwave and hot air treatment (Harlock 1979). While there is heat generated in the host material and the insect's body, the theory is that there is no damage to the foodstuffs.

According to Nelson, particle size and shape of a granular host material could influence lethal exposure levels, with the result that shielding may occur, thus favouring insect survival. Moisture content of the host material may also influence effectiveness. He suggests that insects subjected to sublethal exposures could survive better in materials of high moisture content where they can regain lost moisture. Also noted is the fact that an insect in close contact with a host material may survive brief exposures to higher temperatures, if the heat developing in the insect can be transferred rapidly to the host material (Nelson 1973). Nelson states that adult insects are, in general, more susceptible to control by RF exposure than are the immature stages. As well, species vary in their susceptibility to control by RF exposure.

Pinniger states that "insects alone can survive quite long periods of intensive microwave radiation" (Pinniger 1989, 29) and notes the risks of localized heating causing damage.

In Brezner's studies, insects (adults and larvae of dermestid beetles and adults of tenebrionid beetles) were placed in clear gelatin capsules which were then placed into a cavity carved into the centre of a 3.5 cm hardcover volume. The 50% lethal time varied between 49.6 and 53.4 seconds at medium power (639 watts), depending on the species. A 99% extermination rate was reported at 67.3 to 77 seconds (Brezner 1988).

Overall, the effectiveness of microwave treatment is dependent upon the potential of the insect and the host material for absorbing microwaves. The efficiency of the treatment is dependent upon the intensity and frequency of the radiation, as well as the physical, chemical and dielectrical properties of the insect and the host material (Nelson and Whitney 1960).

The effects of microwaves on fungi and bacteria appears to be minimal. According to the results of a soil treatment study by Ou, Rothwell and Mesa (Brezner 1988) some sterilization could be achieved with high powered and extended (15 minutes) repeated (3x) exposure.

A major disadvantage of microwaves is that they are reported to have a limited penetration of several milimeters. With regard to book materials, this fact was demonstrated by Brezner who stated that "thickness of the sample [book] was inversely proportional to the kill" (Brezner 1988). In food they are reported to penetrate to a depth of about 2 - 4 cm.

6.4.5.2 Effect on Books and Other Materials

The effects of microwaves on the constituent materials of books and other collections are largely unknown. Clearly there are risks involved, the major concern being localized heating that may result in fire, sparking and softening of adhesives. References to library materials are to be found in 6.4.4.5 Pre-Treatment Procedures. Other damage and deterioration effects are yet to be identified.

The CNRS study concluded that drying ability did not depend on speed of the conveyor belt (too slow a speed could overheat paper at the end of the cycle) and that the drying ability did not depend on power. On the other hand, rate of drying depended on power. An acceptable microwave power allows for a relatively short drying time (4 - 5 minutes) without considerable elevation of the final temperature of the dry paper; and the type of paper is affected only slightly the drying mechanism. The weight of the paper modified in a small way the drying time. It was reported that microwaves were able to dry paper effectively in several minutes and did not damage dry paper, if treated one page at a time or multiple pages of 10-20 sheets. Microwave drying by this method only partially dehydrated the paper since there is selective absorption of the microwaves by water. All lost moisture was regained when the paper was returned to an appropriate environment. Overheating was not considered to be a problem when one sheet of paper was subjected to a microwave field of 200-800 watts. Using their microwave dryer, it was noted that a lowering of power by 50% from 800 watts to 400 watts only reduced the speed of drying by about 30%. It was concluded that drying at 400 watts was appropriate, moreso because the surface temperature of the paper stayed fairly low (about 35° C). It was noted that metal attachments (staples, clips, fasteners) could be problematic and that metal oxide inks were not. The effect on gilding was not studied. (Brandt and Berteaud 1987)

A study at the Centre de recherches sur la conservation des documents graphiques in Paris used the CNRS microwave dryer and concluded that water-soaked photographs in relatively good condition could be dried by microwave under appropriate conditions (Gillet and Garnier 1990).

Damage to wool at short exposure times (2450 MHz for 4 minutes) was identified as minimal in the form of slight colour changes. Longer exposure times (10 minutes) caused shrinkage and yellowing (Reagan 1982). Herbarium specimens may become embrittled, and resins may volatilize (Stansfield 1985).

Given the limitations and hazards identified to date, it appears that microwave disinfestation could only be applicable to contemporary materials, of limited value (informational only, not artifactual) and limited thickness. Treatment of sheet materials in unbound format might work well. Some papers, i.e. recycled, would be problematic as well as leathers, certain plastics and adhesives. The known effects would no doubt preclude use of microwave treatment in many institutions.

6.4.5.3 Safety and Effect on Personnel

While not as familiar to people as freezers, microwave ovens and their operation are well known to many. Microwave treatment would probably be a fairly straightforward procedure. However, there are hazards associated with the accidental microwaving of metals and monitoring would be critical. Regular inspections regarding radiation emissions must be made. No chemicals are introduced or believed to be created, thus there is no effect direct or indirect on human health and safety or that of the environment.

6.4.5.4 Effect on Library Operations

Capacity of available domestic microwaves varies from 0.4 cubic feet to 1.4 cubic feet. Actual exposure turn-around time would appear to be quick, but preselection may be extensive and laborious. Depending on materials identified as being unsuitable for treatment, considerable resources could be expended and limited treatment would be accomplished.

Brezner noted in his experiments, that as the number of volumes in the microwave was increased, the time required to achieve 99% kill also increased. Thickness of the materials to be treated is also important, and was found to be inversely proportional to kill (Brezner 1989).

6.4.6 COSTS

The total cost of microwave treatment would vary considerably depending on a number of factors:

- Cost of purchase of equipment and attendant operating and maintenance costs.

- Cost of staff time to retrieve, pre-select, prepare, treat, clean, reshelve and monitor collections, as well as documentation.

The costs of domestic microwave ovens vary considerably depending upon power, oven capacity and other features. The following costs are based on product literature and discussion with vendors:

[Note: $1 Canadian (CDN.) equals approximately $0.85 U.S.]

	Estimated 1991 $ CDN.
■ Small (compact or sub-compact) - 0.4 to 0.6 cubic feet, 500 watts	150-200
■ Medium - 0.8 to 1.0 cubic feet, 600-800 watts	200-300
■ Large - 1.1 - 1.4 cubic feet, 700 - 800 watts	320 and up

6.4.7 BENEFITS AND RISKS

The benefits and risks of microwave treatment are summarized as follows:

- **No real development/advancement of technology for library application.**
Knowledge of library applications is extremely limited. No library or archives is known to use this method.

- **Elimination of toxic chemical problems.**
  Microwaving avoids the problems of toxic chemical use, storage and disposal. No treatment chemical residues/by-products in collections.

- **Minor hazards to human health and safety.**
  Operation of equipment presents minor radiation risk. No hazard to users of treated collections materials.

- **Operation of equipment does not require certification/registration, etc.**
  The application of microwave treatment for the purpose of disinfestation is not covered by legislation.

- **Effective disinfestation of insects may be possible.**
  Treatment may be effective although the specific parameters for treatment and insect species and life stage effects remain to be determined. Limited penetration of microwaves restricts effectiveness.

- **Minimal disinfestation effect on fungi.**
  Microwave treatment is not considered effective against fungi.

- **Post-treatment residual protection against reinfestation.**
  None is provided. Collections must be returned to conditions of good storage.

- **Detrimental effects on library collections exist.**
  Identification of the effects is incomplete; however, damages have been identified.

- **Limited application for library collections.**
  There are limits with regard to the type and size of materials that could be usefully, safely and effectively treated.

- **Improbable use as a preventive measure.**
  Treatment parameters need to be identified.

- **Potentially widely available process.**
  Microwave treatment could be readily undertaken in-house. No external commercial operations are known to exist for library application.

- **Application by library staff.**
  Equipment is familiar to staff. Highly specialized and extensive training is unnecessary.

- **Minimal pre- and post-treatment procedures.**
  Depending on nature of collection, preselection may or may not be required.

- **Rapid turn-around time for minor infestation.**
  In event of minor infestation, materials could be treated and returned to users extremely quickly. Major infestation could be problematic due to requirements for preselection and the limited capacity of existing microwave ovens. Development of conveyor belt systems could expand treatment capabilities.

- **Low cost.**
  Per item cost would be extremely low based on the use of available commercial/consumer ovens. Overall costs would escalate according to the need for preselection.

- **Additional functions.**
  Potential for use in drying collections.

6.4.8   FURTHER RESEARCH

Knowledge of the effects and experience with the application of microwave treatment to library collections are currently very limited. Results to date appear to be positive enough to indicate that the process may have some potential for library application; however, a substantial number of hazards and constraints have already been identified experimentally. It is likely that research efforts will focus on other non-chemical disinfestation treatments with more immediate benefits and wider flexibility of application.

Research is required in a number of areas:

- The effects of microwaves on the constituent materials of library collections.

- Penetration of microwaves in books and stacked sheet materials.

- Effects and efficiency on life stages of various insect species.

- Effects and efficiency on developmental stages of various fungi.

- Use of conveyer belt microwave systems.

6.5   MODIFIED ATMOSPHERES

6.5.1   DESCRIPTION

While used extensively in the agricultural and food industries, the use of modified atmospheres applied to the disinfestation of the collections of cultural institutions is new. A variety of approaches may be used - decreased oxygen concentrations, increased carbon dioxide concentrations in air, atmospheres of inert gases like nitrogen or combinations thereof. The effects on organisms are varied (hyperventilation, asphyxiation, desiccation); however, it is known that these modified atmospheres can provide effective disinfestation of insects, but will not kill fungi. In the case of carbon dioxide, a 5% increase in concentration in air causes a 300% increase in respiration in insects. Modified atmospheres can be applied using various methods or systems including traditional vacuum fumigation chambers, fumigation bubbles, bags of low permeability, sealed boxes, etc.

6.5.2   HISTORY OF USE

The use of modified or controlled atmospheres is an adaptation of the practice of hermetic storage which has been used for centuries as a means of preserving stored food products. The food products were generally sealed in underground pits. The respiration of the commodity plus that of any insects depletes the oxygen to a level that asphyxiates the insects. The reduced level of oxygen also protects the commodity from fungal attack and preserves it over a longer period of time (Davis and Jay 1983).

Over the last twenty years, extensive interest has been shown in the practical application of various modified atmospheres for the protection of stored grains, food products and other goods. In Australia, the United States and other countries, carbon dioxide or nitrogen is used in sealed granaries. Use of low oxygen for packaged foods and other products is widespread. Studies have also been undertaken to determine the effectiveness of methods for transit situations, i.e. hopper cars and freight containers. In the field of stored products, extensive research has been done on the efficacy of atmospheres of differing composition.

In recent years, testing on a variety of pests found in museums, libraries and archives has been undertaken. Results appear to have varied somewhat; however, modified atmospheres show considerable promise as a useful method.

Reports of use of modified atmospheres for disinfestation of collections in cultural institutions are not extensive:

- The North Atlantic Region of National Parks Service in the United States has used carbon dioxide (CO_2) and found that it works effectively on dermestids but not anobiids (The Getty Conservation Institute Newsletter 1988).

- Ipswich Museums reports the use of the Rentokil® Group Plc "fumigation bubble" with methyl bromide, as well as high concentrations of CO_2 for the treatment of natural history collections. A first test was conducted with objects and test insects. After four weeks the insects were found to be alive due to low CO_2 concentrations. A second test was conducted over a three week period. CO_2 was maintained at 60% within the bubble and after three weeks, various life stages of a number of insects, except one larva were found to be dead. Also, briefly mentioned in the report are other successful uses of carbon dioxide. These include the treatment of another natural history collection and a cellar of vintage champagne! (Enwistle and Pearson 1989)

- Rentokil® Group Plc has recently completed further experimental tests on insects and mite pests of stored food and other materials using CO_2. As a result of the study, it is concluded that methyl bromide and phosphine are the best all round fumigants. However, for specialist applications such as the preservation of collections, carbon dioxide has a major role to play provided it can be utilized to best advantage. Field trials using a 60% atmosphere of CO_2 in the "fumigation bubble" have been undertaken over the past two years. A variety of materials have been successfully treated (using an unheated application system) including books, textiles, photographs etc. (Smith and Newton 1991)

- The H.F. Dupont Winterthur Museum in Delaware purchased a Rentokil® "fumigation bubble" in early 1991. A number of suspected infestations in textiles and wooden furniture with upholstery have been treated with CO_2. As far as is known, the treatments have been successful and no damaging effects to the collections have been noted. (Carlson 1992)

- The Houston Museum has used CO_2 in their Rentokil® "fumigation bubble" since the summer of 1991. The preventive treatment of furniture, paintings and boxed textiles is considered successful and no damage to materials was seen. (Hastings 1992)

- The National Museum of Science and Technology in Ottawa has used CO_2 in a Rentokil® "fumigation bubble" for the treatment of active infestations (clothes moths and carpet beetles) in their carriage collections since early summer 1991. The fumigations were considered successful and no damage to the carriages was noted. Post-treatment monitoring with traps was undertaken with no evidence of further infestation. (Warren 1992)

- The Provincial Archives of Manitoba in Canada has converted a vacuum freeze-dry chamber and now uses CO_2, instead of EtO carried in CO_2, for the disinfestation of bound and sheet materials. Conversion of the chamber was undertaken several years ago and it is reported that all life stages of insects in treated collections appear to have been killed, primarily silverfish and firebrats. The chamber is operated in freeze-dry mode with a vacuum. With the CO_2, the system acts as a combination suffdcant and desiccant. Studies have not been undertaken so far, but no changes have been observed in treated collections. No information is currently available on temperature and RH during treatment. (Dalley 1990)

- The Archive of Reino de Galicia, La Coruña, Spain has been using nitrogen (N_2) with Ageless® oxygen absorber under temperature and RH control in plastic bags of low permeability for the treatment of paper documents highly infested by insects of the genera *Anobium* and *Lyctus*. This treatment is considered to be an experiment-in-progress and had been in operation, in August 1990 for one year. Preliminary results indicate 100% effectiveness. Further treatment experiments are in progress (Valentin 1990). These include the use of nitrogen at various environmental conditions in various chambers, as well as comparative studies using N_2, CO_2 and combined N_2/CO_2 (Valentin 1990; Valentin and Preusser 1990; Valentin 1991).

- Rust and Kennedy (1991) report that The Getty Conservation Institute and the University of California, Riverside, entered into an agreement in 1989 to jointly examine the feasibility of insect eradication by means of inert atmospheres. Pure nitrogen with Ageless® oxygen absorber in acrylic chambers was tested on all life stages of 8 species of insects. It was concluded that nitrogen atmospheres can be effectively used for museum and archive pest control.

- Another recent development is the use of oxygen absorbers for the purpose of insect disinfestation in museum collections. A study of the use of Ageless® as a practical means of generating low oxygen atmospheres was recently completed and was considered successful in the eradication of four museum pests. Further research and development of this experimental method is under way (Gilberg 1990). A joint evaluation of Ageless® and its application for museums between Mitsubishi, the Australian Museum in Sydney and the Canadian Conservation Institute is being planned (Grattan 1988).

Note: Ageless® is one of the most widely used oxygen absorbers distributed under its registered trade name by the Mitsubishi Gas Chemical Co. of Japan. Different types and sizes of Ageless® are available depending on the material and the amount of oxygen to be absorbed. Also available is an oxygen indicator product called Ageless-Eye® that is used in tablet form. Ageless® presents no toxicity problems and reduces oxygen in an air-tight container down to 0.01% (100 ppm) or less. The major ingredient is powdered active iron oxide. (Mitsubishi 1987)

6.5.3   PROCESS

In summary, the modified atmosphere process for a generally larger scale application, that is, in a fumigation chamber or bubble, consists of five stages:

1.   Pre-treatment procedures.
     Identification and documentation of nature and extent of infestation.
     Quarantine of infested collection.
     Transport of materials to in-house facility.
     Loading of materials in treatment chamber, e.g. fumigation bubble, vacuum chamber, etc.
     Complete site preparation and set-up procedures as appropriate.

2. Start-up phase.
 Air is evacuated by pulling vacuum.
 CO_2, N_2, etc. is introduced into chamber.

3. Exposure/Extermination.
 Desired atmosphere concentration, temperature and RH are maintained.
 Monitor to verify and control time/temperature/gas concentration/vacuum/ pressure and equipment operation.

4. Recovery phase.
 Vacuum is released.
 CO_2, N_2 is discharged and aeration of chamber is completed.

5. Post-treatment procedures.
 Remove materials from treatment chamber to quarantine area (live insects or new emergence).
 Determine effectiveness of treatment.
 Examine and assess condition of materials.
 Monitor effectiveness of treatment in quarantine where necessary.
 Remove insect remains, debris, etc.
 Transport materials back to conditions of good storage.
 Complete documentation record.
 Adapt process where necessary.

The modified atmosphere process for a smaller scale operation, that is, in bags of low permeability, consists of four stages. This method is still in the developmental/pilot project stage, and may also be applicable to medium-large scale operations (larger items or large volume of smaller items).

1. Pre-treatment procedures.
 Identification and documentation of nature and extent of infestation.
 Quarantine of infested collection.
 Bagging and sealing of materials with oxygen scavenger and indicator.
 OR
 Bagging, purging with nitrogen and sealing of materials with oxygen scavenger.

2. Exposure/Extermination.
 Desired atmosphere concentration, temperature and RH are maintained.
 Monitor to verify and control time/temperature/relative humidity/atmosphere concentration.

3. Post-treatment procedures.
   Open and remove materials from bags in quarantine area.
   Determine effectiveness of treatment.
   Examine and assess condition of materials.
   Isolate materials where necessary to monitor effectiveness of treatment.
   Remove insect remains, debris, etc.
   Transport materials back to conditions of good storage.
   Complete documentation record.
   Adapt process where necessary.

The treatment of collections using modified atmospheres was found to be reported for use only in-house or on-site by institution personnel. It may, however, be possible to arrange for treatment at a commercial facility, or on a cooperative basis.

6.5.4 REQUIREMENTS

6.5.4.1 Legislation

In some countries, the use of CO_2 for the purpose of disinfestation is covered by government legislation. Currently, CO_2 is not registered for use as a fumigant in Canada, although experimental permits for research purposes for various chemical and nonchemical processes can be granted. In the U.S., registration of CO_2 for the purpose of fumigation is not currently required.

No legislation is known to exist regarding the use of N_2, Argon (Ar) or oxygen absorbers for the purpose of disinfestation of library collections.

6.5.4.2 Equipment/Facility

A number of different ways of modifying an atmosphere exist. Various methods of applying the processes have been reported. Requirements vary depending on the method of application.

■ DeCesare (1990) reports the use of Ar in an airtight container such as a 33-gallon plastic trash can. He also suggests the use of plastic bags or enclosed wheeled carts. No details of his study were provided in the report.

■ Dalley (1990) uses a vacuum freeze-dry fumigation chamber converted for use with carbon dioxide. Conversion was reportedly straightforward (gas supply line fittings were changed) as the chamber was designed for use with EtO in CO_2. Conversion of a chamber designed for EtO in freon may be more difficult. The chamber has a heater for the gas, automatic regulators, programmable controls and its own ventilation system. The original chamber was built as a prototype unit and its capacity is 140 cubic feet. It is used with six wheeled carts each having 24 fixed shelves.

- Enwistle and Pearson (1988, 1989), and Child (1988, 1991) reported on the use of the "fumigation bubble" introduced by Rentokil® Group Plc in 1988. The bubble chamber is a squat pouffe in shape consisting of a base sheet with a raised lip to which a plastic PVC (reinforced with polyester net) or laminated aluminum top cover is sealed to the base with a gas tight zip assembly. This equipment folds flat for easy storage and transportation. The bubble can be made to a volume of 60 m³ with an internal supporting frame, the standard one having a volume of 30 m³. Non-return valves, gas samplers and other environmental control systems are fitted into the base sheet.

The gas-tight bubble is filled with a fumigant gas by means of a gas dispenser including an air pump to create a partial vacuum which speeds up and improves efficiency of the process. Methyl bromide, phosphine and carbon dioxide have been used successfully. The bubble has been modified to permit the effective use of CO_2 (Smith and Newton 1991) - an automatic control unit carries up to eight 7 kg cylinders of CO_2 which connect to a single manifold. The unit (connected to combined CO_2 monitor and thermostat) monitors and records gas concentration and temperature throughout fumigation and holds the preset parameters. The unit can control temperatures between ambient and 45° C. There is also now available a recirculating heater that reduces exposure time. A plasticized aluminum cover has been designed for use where it is necessary to insulate the bubble and retain the heat. The bubbles have a predicted working life of at least five years and can also be used for the purpose of quarantine. Modifications for the purpose of dehumidification are planned.

The bubble can be sited indoors or outside, and hoses up to 100 m in length can be connected to the system to dispense the gas/fumigant at a distance. Special gas canisters can be fitted to the suction side to absorb fumigants.

Also reported for experimental purposes by Rentokil® Group Plc was the use of 35 litre high density polyethylene drums with CO_2. The drums set up for treatment contained glass jars of cultures separated by aluminum mesh shelving. Spigots for gassing and sampling were contained in the sealed lid. (Smith and Newton 1991)

- Valentin and Preusser (1990) reported their experiments in the use of nitrogen in a sealed plastic box and a bag of plasticized aluminum of low permeability. In the case of the former, a simple system was designed as follows:

The contaminated objects were placed in a sealed case purged with nitrogen, the flow of which was controlled by a split flow regulator. Nitrogen was humidified and mixed with dry nitrogen and purged through the chamber. A filter on the chamber exhaust retained any possible microbiological contamination. A dew point hygrometer and an oxygen analyzer were used to monitor microenvironmental fluctuations.

In both cases; the oxygen absorber Ageless® was used to react with oxygen stemming from possible leaks in the bag. It is reported that chambers made of various materials (metal and glass), and plastic bags of very low permeability are being tested.

- Valentin (1990, 1991{a}) further reported on studies of the use of nitrogen for the treatment of infested collections using three systems: hermetically-sealed plastic (polyethylene terephthalate) bags of low permeability with the oxygen absorber Ageless®; an experimental stainless steel chamber (750 x 500 x 500 cm) with a glass window equipped with temperature, RH and oxygen sensors; and a traditional fumigation vacuum chamber of 3,105 litres, with computerized controls for temperature, RH, vacuum and pressure.

Based on the results of these experiments, the treatment using nitrogen in the plastic bags is now being applied to an infestation in the Archive of La Reino de Galicia, La Coruña, Spain.

- Rust and Kennedy (1991) reported experiments in the use of nitrogen in hermetically-sealed acrylic chambers. The design of the humidity conditioning and monitoring equipment was similar to that described by Valentin and Preusser (1990). Each chamber also contained a saturated magnesium nitrate solution to maintain RH and Ageless® oxygen absorber. Insects in various life stages were exposed in open containers. Also investigated was the mortality of insects in artificially-infested items. Woodboring insects were placed in screened vials in wooden blocks. Non-woodboring insects were placed in vials submerged in jars covered with packed flour.

- Gilberg (1990) reported on the use of the Ageless® oxygen scavenger in sealed bags of high barrier plastic laminate. The bags were prepared from two sheets of polyvinylidene chloride coated, biaxially oriented nylon. The edges were heat sealed along four sides. In addition to cultures of various life stages of common museum pests, each bag contained a packet of Ageless Z-200® and Ageless-Eye® along with a RH indicator card. The bags were placed inside glass jars and placed in a convection oven. The oxygen content of the bags was measured using a food bag sampling gun.

6.5.4.3 Staff/Operator

The number of staff needed and the training requirements would vary depending on the method and system used to create a modified atmosphere. The operation and maintenance of a vacuum chamber requires specialized training. The requirement for the use of the fumigation bubble would be somewhat less complex; however, the use of pressure and compressed gases, whatever the application, necessitates certain safety procedures. This would also apply to the use of low permeability bags with nitrogen. The use of oxygen absorbers in low permeability bags would require the least amount of technical expertise in its application; however, staff time for preparation would be increased.

6.5.4.4 Temperature/Relative Humidity/Time/Other

Many studies have been undertaken regarding modified atmospheres applied to food storage. There are relatively few references in the literature regarding use on collections in cultural institutions or experimental studies on museum, library, and archival pests. The requirements vary according to the method of modifying the atmosphere and the equipment used.

■ According to the Rentokil® Group Plc "Fumigation Bubble" Operation and Instruction Manual, (B&G Equipment Co. 1989) the length of time under gas in the bubble is normally 15 days and concentration is normally 60% CO_2. The recirculating heater, now available, reduces the normal exposure time to 4 days. It is noted that the bubble is capable of retaining high concentrations of nitrogen for long periods but that the very long exposure periods and high concentrations required usually preclude its use. It was further noted that overheating of the bubble dispenser system in very hot climates can occur.

Enwistle and Pearson's (1989) tests at Ipswich Museums with carbon dioxide in the fumigation bubble were problematic at first and were attributed to low CO_2 concentration. Test insects (larvae, pupal and adult stages of various species) placed with the natural history specimens being treated were alive after four weeks, although their growth had been arrested. A second test was undertaken. This time the concentration of CO_2 within the bubble was measured and by refilling was maintained at 60%. The temperature was kept between $10°$ and $17°$ C, measured with a thermohygrograph inside the bubble. No RH information was provided. After 3 weeks, all insects except one larva were found to be dead. All test insects were kept under observation - none of the insects revived nor did the eggs hatch. A total of at least 259 kgs of CO_2 was used. It was determined that the membrane of the bubble was permeable to CO_2 and the coupling attachment for gas introduction was unsuitable for CO_2. As noted, Rentokil® Group Plc has since made design alternations so that CO_2 may be effectively used. Other treatments reported in Enwistle and Pearson's tests do not include time, concentration, temperature, etc., data.

■ Smith and Newton (1991) reported on the results of experimental studies using CO_2 in drums. At $15°$ C, 14 days exposure to CO_2, 100% mortality was reported for a number of species of mites, lice, moths, cockroaches and beetles except *Sitophilus oryzae* (rice weevil) which required 28 days exposure. At $23°$ C, 100% mortality was achieved on exposure to CO_2 for one to four days exposure, except for the rice weevil and *Anthrenus verbasci* (varied carpet beetle) which required 14 days CO_2 exposure at $25°$ C. Exposure to CO_2 at $35°$ C for four days controlled most species. Fourteen days exposure at $35°$ C was required to effect 100% mortality on *T. putrescentiae* (mite), *T. granarium* (Khapra beetle) and *A. punctatum* (common furniture beetle). Mean concentrations of CO_2 were generally within 5% of the desired 60%. Relative humidity was maintained at about 75%. It was concluded that the results achieved were broadly consistent with published data reviewed by Annis in 1987.

Smith and Newton further describe the modified "Fumigation Bubble" field trials. Over the past two years, a wide variety of materials (including leather- and parchment-bound books and photographs) have been successfully treated in a 60% CO_2 concentration. Further work is planned to confirm the results of these initial studies and to determine parameters for the treatment of various types of collections.

- Three Rentokil® "Fumigation Bubbles" were identified as being in operation in North America (See 6.5.2 History of Use):

The H. F. Dupont Winterthur Museum treatments have been undertaken in 60% CO_2, at room temperature over 2 weeks. Temperature and RH are not currently monitored. (Carlson 1992)

The Houston Museum treatments have been undertaken in 65% CO_2, at room temperature over 100 days. Temperature and RH are not known. (Hastings 1992)

The National Museum of Science and Technology (Ottawa) treatments have been undertaken in 60% CO_2, at 20° C and 50%-60% RH over 10 days. (Warren 1992)

All treatments in these institutions were considered successful.

- Gilberg (1989) studied the effects of low oxygen atmospheres on a number of pests common to museums including clothes moths and a number of species of beetles. Insect cultures (different developmental stages of *Anthrenus vorax, Stegobium paniceum, Lasioderma serricorne, Tineola bisselliella and Lyctus brunneus*) were exposed to a mixture of 0.42% oxygen with nitrogen at a constant temperature of 30° C and a relative humidity of 65% - 70%. 30° C was chosen because of the increased effectiveness of low oxygen concentrations with an increase in temperature. It was also considered to be the safe maximum temperature for a museum object. After exposure of one, two and three weeks mortality was found to be 100%. Subsequent observations revealed no evidence of delayed hatching.

Gilberg (1991) further discusses the application of low O_2 atmospheres in terms of these 1989 trials. He states that for 100% mortality, museum objects must be exposed to an O_2 concentration of 0.4% or less, at a temperature greater than or equal to 30° C for at least three weeks. He concludes that shorter exposure time would likely effect 100% mortality, but that an exact determination, using these trial results, cannot be made.

More quantitative studies were undertaken by Gilberg (1990) involving all developmental stages of four of the species tested in 1989. This work yielded similar results following purging with nitrogen gas (less than 0.5% oxygen) for 3 weeks at 30° C.

Gilberg (1990) also studied low oxygen disinfestation using Ageless® oxygen absorber as a practical means of creating an inert atmosphere. Ageless® is an iron-based oxygen absorber and is, according to product literature, capable of reducing the oxygen concentration in an air-tight bag or container down to 0.01% (100 ppm) or less. It will maintain this level indefinitely depending on the permeability of the packaging. Ageless® is available in different types and packet sizes depending on the water activity of the packaged material and the amount of oxygen to be absorbed.

Gilberg's experiments with insect cultures of different life stages of *Anthrenus vorax*, *Stegobium paniceum*, *Lasioderma serricorne* and *Tineola bisselliella* demonstrated 100% mortality after three treatments in sealed plastic bags containing Ageless® Z-200 and Ageless-Eye®. The oxygen concentration was maintained at less than 1% (measured by a portable oxygen analyzer, subsequent gas chromatography indicated less than 0.05%) and temperature at 30° C, RH at 60%. Further studies are under way on reduction of the bag air volume by evacuation and nitrogen purging.

- Valentin and Preusser (1990), in their studies, examined the effectiveness of a nitrogen atmosphere for the control of the fruit fly, *Drosophila melanogaster*, as an experimental model. The results obtained were then applied to the treatment of cellulose materials including books and documents infested by *Cryptotermes brevis*, termites. It was determined that a nitrogen atmosphere at 75% relative humidity, 20° - 25° C, and 0.5% oxygen concentration was effective in eradicating 100% of all the life stages of *D. melanogaster* after 80 hours (3.3 days) incubation. With the same oxygen level, the combination of a low relative humidity (40%) and a high temperature (30° C) was 100% effective after 30 hours (1.25 days) incubation. It was found that no significant increase in mortality was found on control populations in air at temperatures lower than 35° C and relative humidities of 40% - 75%. A nitrogen atmosphere was also found to be effective in eliminating 100% of the termite, *Cryptotermes brevis*, in contaminated wood pieces exposed to 40% relative humidity and 25° C at oxygen levels lower than 1% for three weeks incubation.

Valentin and Preusser conclude that the combination of high temperature and low relative humidity during treatment has a drastic effect on the mortality of insects exposed to oxygen exclusion. They further reference Lambert's studies that show that nitrogen can diffuse relatively rapidly into porous materials in order to replace the oxygen and that oxygen absorbers can maintain oxygen levels lower than 1.1 ppm for many weeks.

- Further studies by Valentin (1990) used various systems for exposure of cellulose materials (books, bundles of papers) infested with the furniture beetle, *Anobium punctatum*, to a nitrogen atmosphere. Bags of low permeability were purged with nitrogen at 250 ml/min (to replace the air) at 35% RH and 30° C over 8 hours. Ageless® oxygen absorber was used to maintain an average 0.9% O_2 concentration during treatment. Parallel experiments were undertaken in a metallic chamber. And a vacuum chamber with computerized controls was also used. Valentin concludes that "using plastic bags of low permeability ... 100% mortality was achieved in all insects placed in books which were treated in a chamber purged with a nitrogen atmosphere and incubated for 10 days" (Valentin 1990, 822). Identical results were achieved for the materials treated in the metallic chamber. Preliminary testing in the vacuum chamber shows that operation time for 100% mortality is reduced by approximately 40% at conditions of 30° C, 35% RH, 1.5 g/cm² vacuum and nitrogen introduced at 1 kg/cm² pressure.

A pilot project is currently under way at the Archive of Reino de Galicia, La Coruña, Spain to further this work on nitrogen atmospheres in low permeability plastic bags. Preliminary results showed that bundles of papers infested by *Coleoptera* can be successfully treated in bags purged with a nitrogen atmosphere (250 ml/min), under 30% RH, 30° C for 10 hours and 20 days incubation. Ageless® oxygen absorber was used in each bag. Further experiments are in progress, including the use of a combination of gases such as nitrogen and carbon dioxide - the incubation time might be decreased due to the CO_2 effect of increasing the rate of respiration of insects (Ali Niazee 1971).

- Valentin, Lidstrom and Preusser (1990) recently developed and evaluated a method of microbial control that uses low levels of both oxygen and relative humidity for the treatment and storage of infested materials. The study used a ^{14}C labelled radioactive tracer method to assess the microbial growth of the experiment. Contaminated parchment samples were placed in sealed vials in which the air was replaced by nitrogen and the RH controlled by silica gel. The experimental results obtained showed that a combination of low oxygen and RH levels reduces microbial activity on proteinaceous materials to undetectable levels within relatively short exposure times in a range of oxygen levels 0.1% - 1%, RH lower than 43% at temperatures of 20° - 22° C. The effect of modified atmospheres on other contaminated materials is being investigated.

- Further research by Valentin (1991{a}) used nitrogen in plastic bags and a vacuum chamber to study the effects on *Anobium punctatum, Hylotrupes bajulus, Micobium castaneum and Stegobium paniceum* in paper and wood samples. 100% mortality of all stages of *A. punctatum* was achieved using a nitrogen atmosphere in plastic bags at 30° C, 60% RH, and 0.05% O_2 after five days exposure. The exposure time was reduced to 3 days using a vacuum chamber under identical conditions. Eggs were particularly sensitive to the N_2 treatment at temperatures of 30° - 35° C and 45-50% RH. *H. bajulus* was found to be a species resistant to low oxygen atmospheres - 9 days exposure at 30° C, 50% RH was required to effect 100% larvae mortality. Nitrogen was found to be more effective for eliminating *A. punctatum* and *H. bajulus* in wood than in paper samples. This effect is attributed to the gas accumulation in boreholes and galleries. Archival materials containing *M. castaneum, S. paniceum and A. punctatum* were also effectively treated using inert atmospheres in (0.5% O_2) in plastic bags at low temperatures (22° C) and high RH (67%-70%) for 15 days. It was concluded that inert atmospheres in chambers can effect 100% insect mortality in shorter exposure times of 3 to 5 days.

Valentin (1991{b}) reported that minimum N_2 exposure times for *Anobium punctatum, Micobium castaneum, Stegobium paniceum and Hylotrupes bajulus* had been determined through further testing of each life stage. Highly infested paper and wood samples were used. The conditions of a N_2 atmosphere in plastic bags necessary for 100% mortality in paper (book samples) are 30° C at 40% RH for 3 days. The results of wood sample testing showed that the temperature and time requirements were the same as for the paper samples; however, for both the bag and chamber disinfestation 50% RH was required. It is recommended that 10 days exposure be used for very resistant insects *(Hylotrupes bajulus)* to ensure their eradication.

- Rust and Kennedy (1991) examined the effectiveness of a pure nitrogen atmosphere (oxygen concentration <0.1%) humidified to 55% RH on all life stages of 8 species of insects including firebrats, German cockroaches, various beetles and drywood termites. It was reported that with the exception of *Lasioderma serricorne*, the cigarette beetle, the data show agreement with the results obtained by Valentin (1990). For the tested species, the exposure time to achieve 100% mortality for specimens buried within objects was not substantially greater than specimens exposed in open containers. Buried specimen exposure times varied from 48 to 120 hours, except for the cigarette beetle which required 192 hours. Open container exposure times ranged from 3 hours to 120 hours, except for the cigarette beetle which required 120 to 168 hours. Concentrations of CO_2 less than 20% do not appear to increase the efficacy of nitrogen alone. Future work will involve experiments at different RH and temperatures.

6.5.4.5 Pre-Treatment Procedures

To date, no special pre-treatment preparation of materials has been identified as being necessary for treatment in a chamber or bubble. Treatment in bags of low permeability requires the bagging and sealing of items.

6.5.4.6 Post-Treatment Procedures

To date, no post-treatment procedures have been identified as being necessary except for those activities standard to the completion of any disinfestation treatment - cleaning of materials, evaluation, monitoring and documentation.

6.5.5   RESULTS

6.5.5.1   Effectiveness of Disinfestation

Effective disinfestation of insects may be achieved through the use of different modified atmospheres by a variety of methods. Optimum methods for their application to library collections are not yet fully understood. Modified atmospheres are less effective for the treatment of fungi. While growth may be arrested, suppressed ... the spores of fungi can survive the unfavourable conditions in a state of rest and can remain viable for many years (Brokerhof 1989). However, recent studies into microbial control by low oxygen and low RH environment show considerable promise (Valentin, Lidstrom and Preusser 1990).

As a result of his studies to control stored grain insects, Jay considers CO_2 to be more effective than N_2 in situations where tight sealing is physically impossible or not economically feasible. For while nitrogen has the advantage of initially filling 78% of the interstitial spaces, atmospheric oxygen must be reduced to less than 1% or 2% to obtain effective insect control and maintain at this level many times longer than with CO_2 (Jay 1980; Story 1985). Carbon dioxide is effective at levels as low as 30% - 35%. It is said that a concentration of 60% CO_2 held for four days (or 45% for 5-6 days or 35% for 7 days) at a temperature of 21° C or higher will kill all life stages of most pests (Jay 1971; Story 1985).

In general, atmospheres of about 60% CO_2 are considered to be the most practical for the control of stored product pests (Banks 1979). Concentrations above 60% are not as effective in the extermination of insects and are more difficult to maintain. An exposure to 60% CO_2 at 20° - 29° C for approximately 11 days was determined to serve to control most species of stored product pests in grains (Annis 1987).

Practical experience with CO_2 has been reported using the "fumigation bubble" and a converted vacuum freeze-dry chamber. Disinfestation of various species of insects has been reported to be successful. The use of CO_2 in drums as well as nitrogen in chambers, with and without vacuum, and with an oxygen absorber is also reported to be successful in experimental work. A pilot project using nitrogen and an oxygen absorber in sealed bags is considered successful after one year. Other research using nitrogen and oxygen absorbers in various chambers have been extremely encouraging (Valentin 1990, 1991; Rust and Kennedy 1991). Use of oxygen absorbers alone in sealed bags has also demonstrated effective results.

The parameters for the optimum effectiveness of the application of modified atmosphere systems for the treatment of collections are yet to be conclusively determined. However, the following conclusions can be drawn from the experience and research undertaken to date:

- The effect of temperature and RH on the length of time necessary to obtain good control with modified atmospheres is as important as with conventional fumigants (David and Jay 1983). Exposure time to CO_2 required to kill insects decreases as the temperature increases (Navarro and Jay 1987). Lab studies have also shown that lowering the RH increases the effectiveness of modified atmospheres (Jay et al. 1971).

- Desiccation plays a large role in the mortality of insects when exposed to some modified atmospheres. (Jay and Cuff 1981)

- The same modified atmospheres have different effects on different species and different life stages of each species. (Jay and Pearman 1971)

- Different modified atmospheres show different results on the same species and life stage.

- The age of the species eggs, (larvae, pupae, adults) may influence the lethal effect of modified atmospheres (Valentin 1991).

- CO_2 and N_2 can be effective, one may be more effective in a particular application. N_2 can be used effectively in tightly sealed containers but in non air-tight situations is problematic because the gas concentration must be kept above the effective level of 99%. CO_2 can be used in non air-tight situations because it is effective at around 50% and is very effective at concentrations up to 60%.

- The use of oxygen absorbers shows considerable promise. Studies have shown that insects, regardless of life stage, can be killed completely by maintaining an oxygen-free state for 14 days at room temperature. It was also found that almost all moulds cannot grow under the oxygen-free conditions created by oxygen absorbers.

6.5.5.2 Effect on Books and Other Materials

Modified atmospheres appear to be non-damaging to collections; however, to date, little research has been done in this area. Concern has been expressed as to potential acidification problems resulting from the reaction of carbon dioxide with water in the surrounding atmosphere and/or the material being treated to yield carbonic acid. Sanders (1987) studied the effect of carbon dioxide on the surface pH of four organic materials including several papers. Exposure to CO_2 was for 72 hours at 63% relative humidity. In her tests, there were no changes significant enough to be measured by the pH strips.

According to both Strang and Druzik, the factors involved in CO_2 fumigation argue against CO_2 as a potential risk. These factors include: the relative weakness of carbonic acid as an agent of acidification; the small amount of available water in which CO_2 can dissolve; and the rapid desorption of CO_2 following fumigation. It is concluded that "only 0.16 percent of the dissolved carbon dioxide will form carbonic acid (in an open system) ... the amount of potential acidity contributed during a 60% CO_2 fumigation of book[s] with only ambient moisture content will be minute" (Druzik 1992). (Strang 1992{a})

With regard to the use of nitrogen, Valentin and Preusser conclude that "chemical or physical alternatives in the materials should be reduced to minimal levels" (Valentin and Preusser 1990, 31).

With CO_2 "Bubble Fumigation" appropriate care should be taken when filling and evacuating the CO_2, so as to ensure no physical damage to the collections.

Clearly, modified atmospheres are less reactive than many conventional fumigants; however, the effects of modified atmospheres on the constituent materials of library collections appear to be largely unknown.

6.5.5.3 Safety and Effect on Personnel

The operator risks are limited to short-term toxicity rather than long-term effects from chronic exposure. For example, CO_2 at a concentration of 60% is not safe unless contained in a gas-tight container. Exposure to concentrations near 10% for a few minutes can produce coma and subsequent asphyxiation. Exposure to concentrations of 25% - 30% causes coma and convulsions within one minute. Further exposure can result in death. Use and the venting of CO_2 should be undertaken with appropriate care. Specialized training of personnel is required.

There are no problems of residues for staff or users who handle treated materials.

6.5.5.4 Effect on Library Operations

Practical experience on which to judge the effect on library operations is minimal. Turn-around time for all methods of application will depend largely on the capacity of the chamber/bubble/bag. The standard capacity of the fumigation bubble is 30 m^3 or just under 1,000 cubic feet. Turn-around time would range from four days to three weeks depending on the type of treatment. There is also an advantage in that the bubble can be folded away when not in use and/or transported to other locations.

The capacity of fumigation chambers varies considerably and turn-around would again depend on the type of treatment. The use of plastic bags could be expected to have a more substantive effect on library operations due to the staff resources required for bagging, although this may be largely offset by the low technical nature of the operation.

6.5.6 COSTS

The total cost of treatment by modified atmospheres would vary considerably depending on a number of factors including the method of application.

- Cost of purchase of equipment or retrofit of existing chamber and attendant operating and maintenance costs.

- Cost of supplies including gases, bags, oxygen absorbers.

- Cost of staff time to retrieve, prepare, treat, clean, reshelve and monitor collections, as well as documentation.

The following costs are based on information available in the literature and discussions with various institutions and vendors:

	Estimated 1991 $ CDN.
[Note: $1 Canadian (CDN.) equals approximately $0.85 U.S.]	
■ Fumigation bubble developed by Rentokil® Group Plc. Price in Canada. Price depends on specifications. Note: Bubble is available for rent in the United Kingdom and North America.	9,000 - 10,000
■ Fumigation chamber of capacity approximately 140 cubic feet. Price depends on specifications.	25,000-40,000
■ Retrofit fumigation chamber. Price depends on modifications necessary.	500-5,000
■ Cylinder of CO_2 (22.68 kilograms).	40
N_2 (6.21 cubic meters). Prices based on minimum orders.	45
■ Plastic bags. Price depends on material specifications , purchase in bag form or film sheeting, dimensions and size of order. Dupont Oxybar®4 (0.05, ethylene vinyl alcohol, roll 12¾" x 2,000').	275
Dupont polyvinylidene chloride (roll 12¾" x 2,000').	200
■ Heat sealer. Price depends on specifications.	50-300
■ Mitsubishi Ageless® Z-200. Price based on minimum order of 40 cases, 1,500 packets/carton (@0.064). For smaller orders cost can be as much as double.	3,800

6.5.7   BENEFITS AND RISKS

The benefits and risks of modified atmospheres can be summarized as follows:

- **Moderate development/advancement of technologies for library application.**
  Experiences with library collections are limited. Application methods are in various stages of development.

- **Elimination of toxic chemical problems.**
  Modified atmospheres avoid the problems of toxic chemical use, storage and disposal. No treatment chemical residues/by-products in collections.

- **Operator and/or design/operation of equipment for purpose of disinfestation with certain gases may be legislated/regulated.**
  Certification/registration requirements vary depending upon the country and nature of use.

- **Negligible to moderate hazards to human health and safety.**
  Risks vary widely depending on the process and its method of application.
  Note: Acute short-term toxicity of CO_2.   No hazard to users of treated material.

- **Effective disinfestation of insects.**
  Treatment appears to be effective in killing all life stages of insect species tested. There remain inconsistencies as to recommended treatment parameters.

- **Retardation of growth and activity of fungi.**
  Modified atmospheres alone are not considered an effective disinfestation method for fungi.

- **Post-treatment residual protection against reinfestation.**
  None is provided. Collections must be returned to conditions of good storage.

- **To date, no identified detrimental effects on library collections.**
  It appears that books and documents may be treated without damage. Experience and studies are limited.

- **Potential application to variety of library materials.**
  Modified atmospheres may be applicable to various materials (size, type and format).

- **Potential use as a preventive measure.**
  Modified atmospheres could be used as a preventive measure for incoming collections.

- **Potentially widely available process.**
  Modified atmospheres could be undertaken in-house and on a co-operative basis. No external commercial facilities are known to exist for library application. Considerable flexibility in application exists.

- **Application by library staff.**
  Modified atmospheres could be applied by library staff. Training requirements would vary depending on the process and application method.

- **Minimal pre- and post-treatment procedures.**
  Preparation and post-treatment activities are straightforward and relatively minor. Treatment involving bagging could be labour intensive.

- **Fairly rapid turn-around time.**
  Materials could be treated relatively quickly and made available to users.

- **Low cost.**
  Information is limited but costs appear to be low. Per item cost overall would vary depending on the process and method of application.

- **Additional functions.**
  None identified to date.

6.5.8   FURTHER RESEARCH

Modified atmospheres (reduced O_2 concentrations, increased CO_2 concentrations, gas combinations, etc.) appear to offer several safe, effective and affordable alternatives to chemical disinfestation treatment, although all are in the developmental stage. To date, there has been scant information published on the use of Ar, which being completely inert may have enormous potential for library application.

Research is required in a number of areas:

- The effects of low oxygen/oxygen absorbers, CO_2, N_2, Ar, etc. on the constituent materials of library collections.

- The effects of high CO_2 concentration atmospheres on materials (acidification due to absorption of CO_2 by moisture in materials).

- The comparative effectiveness and operational requirements for CO_2, N_2, low O_2, Ar, etc.

- The effects and efficiency of CO_2, N_2, low O_2, Ar, etc. on the life stages of various insects.

- The effects and efficiency of CO_2, N_2, low O_2, Ar, etc. on the developmental stages of various fungi.

- The penetration of CO_2, N_2, low O_2, Ar, etc. in closely packed materials.

See Note, 6.2.8 Further Research (Deep-Freezing).

7.0   OTHER NONCHEMICAL TREATMENT, CONTROL AND PREVENTION METHODS

7.1   INTRODUCTION

This section briefly discusses other methods of nonchemical treatment, control and prevention. Some of the methods and procedures can be employed in-house with minimal training and cost, and are more applicable to small localized infestations. Other methods have institution-wide implications and require considerable organization and resources. External experts and services will also be required for some applications.

7.2   MECHANICAL

Fungi, as well as insect debris, can be removed by mechanical means using brushes, powdered erasers, tweezers, etc., with the aid of suction, ie. vacuums, minis vacs, vacuum aspiration. These methods are extremely labour intensive and can only be safely used on relatively strong and stable materials. The treatment of fragile materials should be undertaken by a conservator.

The use of such methods also presents an opportunity for spores and possibly eggs and larvae to be widely spread in and beyond the treatment area. It is preferable to undertake such treatments in an isolation room, a fume hood or outside to reduce the health threat to the operator and the risk of contamination of other materials. If using suction devices, disposable paper collection bags should be used with controlled exhaust, such as provided by HEPA (High Efficiency Air Particulate) filtration.

7.3   HEAT

Sterilization by heat, derived from steam or hot air, is one of the oldest, most common and extremely effective methods used in the food industry and medical field to kill bacteria and insects. Heat can be used on a small scale or large scale basis.

It is reported that in most cases, insects will be killed after exposure to hot air at 60° C for at least one hour and that exposure to hot air of 160° C for 120 minutes or 180° C for 30 minutes will kill bacteria. Steam sterilization is usually performed at temperatures of 120° C or 130° C for 20 or 30 minutes respectively. (Brokerhof 1989)

Heat, generally accelerates all processes, including oxidation and thus ageing. It is recognized that paper can become embrittled and other materials are variously sensitive to the dry or humid heat which is applied.

Thermal pest treatment is used for eradication of insects in residential dwellings in several areas of the United States. Heaters with blowers and flexible ducting are used to raise temperatures in the buildings high enough to kill structural and contents pests such as beetles, carpenter ants, termites and cockroaches.

7.4   INSECT-RESISTANT CONTAINERS AND PACKAGING

Insect-resistant storage containers and packaging can provide a measure of protection and have a valuable role to play where spread of an infestation needs to be limited. They may also serve as holding containers during treatment, i.e. freezing, low oxygen or after treatment where controlled observation is required to determine the effectiveness of a treatment.

Many forms of packaging have been developed and studied by the food industry. Some plastics in particular, have shown promise in resisting insects. In an outline of relative resistance to insect penetration of common packaging materials - polyester, polycarbonate and polyurethane were rated excellent, 10-mil polyethylene, polypropylene (biaxially oriented) and polyvinyl chloride (unplasticized) were rated good, 5-mil polyethylene fair and 1-, 2-, 3-, and 4-mil polyethylene poor. Susceptibility to penetration depends on the thickness of the basic film resin, combination of materials, package structure and on species and stage of insects involved (Highland 1984). A packaging film is also more likely to be penetrated by insects if creased or crumpled (Newton 1988).

A number of libraries have reported shrink-wrapping and heat seal bagging collections as a protective measure against infestations and pollution. However, there are major concerns regarding the creation of microclimates which may accelerate ageing processes. Increased local humidities and condensation are possibilities depending on the type of wrap/bag material, the moisture content of the collection when enclosed, etc. This should not be a problem with polyethylene which allows for adequate water vapour and air exchange. Moisture buffering compounds and oxygen scavengers can be used to control the enclosed climate. Additionally, many plastics deteriorate over time releasing gases and other substances that damage paper and other materials.

Other packaging (boxes, envelopes, etc.) constructed of paper or cardboard serve well as protection against pollution, handling, etc., and may resist less aggressive pests. The constituent materials however, also tend to be attractive to insects. Metal and glass containers are generally insect-resistant; however, metal foil wrapping can be pierced by hide and drugstore beetles (Story 1985). In Highland's 1984 review of insect resistance, corrugated paperboard, kraft paper and paper/foil/polyethylene laminate were rated poor.

7.5   BIOLOGICAL CONTROLS

The advantage of biological controls is that they are safe to man and the environment. Many are species specific in their effect and harmless to other organisms. Their disadvantage is that they do not eradicate the infestation, rather reduce the damage to an acceptable level. Extensive research in the agriculture and horticulture fields has demonstrated that certain methods such as pheromones, predators, and sterile males can be effectively used. Others, such as the use of diseases, show little potential against indoor pests.

Little is known about the application of these methods to cultural institutions or their effect on collections. Pheromones, however, have been identified as a possible method for museums. Pheromone traps designed for *Lasioderma serricorne* (F.), the cigarette beetle and *Stegobium paniceum* (L.), the drugstore beetle, are now commercially available (Parker 1991{a}). See Note, 6.2.8 Further Research (Deep-Freezing).

7.6   ENVIRONMENTAL CONTROL AND MODIFICATION

There is no doubt that the vast majority of materials that constitute library collections are vulnerable to the effects of uncontrolled conditions of temperature, relative humidity (RH), light and air quality and to the associated forms of chemical, photochemical, biological and microbiological damage and deterioration. In the case of insects and fungi, infestations can be largely prevented through environmental control or modification. For while insects and fungi thrive in various conditions, most prefer high humidities. Book lice, for example, which feed on microscopic mould in damp library materials, can well be controlled by keeping the RH below 50% (Story 1985, 79). In an environment of continuous low RH (below 35%) book lice will desiccate and die (Parker 1988, 32). Mould spores are, of course, found everywhere and thus maintenance of temperature and RH conditions at levels not conducive to their growth is critical.

While control of the environmental conditions should be the goal of every institution, it is not easily achieved. Environmental standards established for the preservation of paper-based materials are difficult, if not impossible, to maintain on a consistent basis by the vast majority of libraries. Systems which are able to monitor and control both temperature and RH in balance and do so within established parameters are rare. Most institutions depend upon modification of one or more of the factors involved in order to achieve a measure of control. This includes adjustment of the established parameters and/or the use of equipment in order to maintain a balance of temperature and RH. While this approach requires more consistent monitoring and adjustment, it can be equally successful in the control of infestation, except of course in the event of a major disaster.

7.7   FACILITY MANAGEMENT AND MODIFICATION

Institutional policies and procedures with regard to building maintenance, sanitation and general housekeeping can be extremely effective in the prevention and identification of problem situations. Many of the references in the literature have come from the fields of agriculture, horticulture and the food industry; however, in recent years, many of these ideas have come to be applied and adapted for use in cultural institutions. Many of these measures are pure common sense, require limited technical expertise and can be readily applied by most organizations.

Such measures would include:

- Exclusion methods including sealing of entry holes, use of door gaskets and sweepers and automatic door closures.

- Improved sanitation with regard to cleaning and hygiene measures within and external to the building, disposal of garbage, policies re storage and consumption of food.

- Design modifications to allow for easy and efficient cleaning (smooth walls and floors, avoiding horizontal surfaces, space allowance for cleaning under/behind equipment).

- Repellent, non-attractant methods including use of inorganic mulches, non-flowering shrubs and trees and non-attractant sodium vapour external lighting.

- Detection methods such as an insect trapping programme with appropriate selection, placement and maintenance of traps.

7.8   COLLECTION MANAGEMENT AND MAINTENANCE

Collection management and maintenance can play a key role in the prevention, monitoring and detection of infestation. Early warning of the presence of pests is critical to the application of successful control stages. Some of the measures that can be employed are clearly the responsibility of curatorial staff alone, while others require the co-operation of the curatorial, technical, facilities, and support staffs to effect a coordinated comprehensive programme.

Such measures would include:

- Visual examination of materials at point of entry (acquisition, loan, exhibition).

- Cleaning of collections where necessary or on a routine basis, if feasible.

- Isolation/quarantine of collections where necessary.

- Routine inspection of storage, use, and exhibition areas.

- Programme for sitings, submissions, evaluation and documentation.

8.0   CONCLUSIONS

There are now available in various stages of development, a number of nonchemical alternatives for the disinfestation of library materials. The major benefit of all of these is the elimination of toxic chemicals and problems, direct and indirect, resulting from their use. Insects, in general, may be effectively treated by a number of the methods described. The effective eradication of fungi is more difficult. Of the nonchemical alternatives described, high-energy radiation alone can assuredly kill fungi.

There remain many questions to be answered for all processes including:

- Effectiveness on a variety of library pests at various life stages.
- Effectiveness on a variety of fungi at various developmental stages.
- Effects on a variety of constituent materials of library collections.
- Optimum parameters for application of these processes.

At the moment, deep-freezing offers the maximum benefits with minimal risks. It is clean, rapid and a process that is widely available. It is flexible in application and can be used by institutions with varying requirements. The equipment used is familiar, non-threatening to staff, and its operation straightforward with little risk to the operator. From a practical point of view, materials require relatively little preparation, although bagging can be labour intensive. The process can be undertaken in-house and costs following initial purchase of the equipment are minimal. Experience with application to library, archival and museum materials goes back 14 years and results are reported to be successful given appropriate low temperatures and exposure times. No damaging effects to library materials have been identified and a variety of types of collections can be treated safely and quickly. Further research needs to be done regarding optimum conditions for various species of insects and the effects of freezing on library materials. A freezer has the additional advantage of being able to stabilize water-wetted materials, and the design of some units allows for the drying of wet materials.

High-energy radiation is the only alternative to chemical control for the eradication of fungi. It is also effective on insects. At this point, gamma radiation is the only high-energy radiation process which has been reported for use to disinfest collections, other than on an experimental basis, although other processes may prove to be useful. It is not a process that can be generally undertaken in-house. Its operation is highly regulated and should be undertaken by an appropriate commercial facility. It is a clean, and extremely rapid process; however, public concern over the use of radiation in general may preclude its use in some areas of the world. Reported costs for treatment are reasonable and in some countries, the process would be widely available. The major disadvantage of this process is that, based on studies to date, the dose required to effect eradication of mould causes damage to cellulose and other materials. The lower doses required to eradicate insects may also be damaging.

While the long-term effects of this type of radiation are largely unknown, it is believed that the degradation processes, once initiated, continue on after treatment. Limited experiences cited in the literature indicate its successful application to library materials; however, given the known effects, its use may be more suitable for situations where information content of the items is critical or, in extreme cases, where materials are severely and extensively infested.

Low-energy radiation (microwaves) appears to be effective against insects and its low cost, wide availability, rapidity and ease of application have definite appeal. However, the limited penetrating abilities of microwaves greatly restrict the usefulness of this method. It has major disadvantages including the production of heat during treatment and the small volume of materials that can be treated at one time. Damaging effects to library materials have been identified and existing knowledge of the consequences of treating materials is limited. Little research on its effectiveness on various insects species has been done nor optimum parameters for treatment. There is no evidence to suggest practical experience with this process in a library application.

Modified atmospheres offer a new, promising and effective alternative to the chemical treatment of insects; however, experience to date with library materials is limited. A number of advantages can be identified, and the risks at this point appear minimal. Modified atmosphere treatment is clean and the process can be effected in various ways (CO_2, N_2, low O_2) using different systems (fumigation chamber, bubble, bags of low permeability). Thus, it may prove to be applicable to a wide variety of situations and has the advantage, in the case of the bubble, of temporary use and then storage, as well as use outdoors. Risk to the operator is limited, i.e. acute toxicity of CO_2. The use of bags offers considerable flexibility in treating different sizes and volumes of materials. Moreover, the equipment necessary may be a modification of an existing chamber. No damaging effects to library materials have been identified and it appears that a variety of types of collections could be treated safely and rapidly. Ongoing costs are not extensive. Further research needs to be done on the optimum conditions for treatment including various compositions of the atmospheres. As well, information is needed on its effects of the constituent materials of library collections.

Each of the nonchemical processes described has identified advantages, as well as disadvantages inherent to their nature and method of application. None, given our current knowledge of their effects and requirements, is a panacea. Their use must be made with a full understanding of the risks involved, both short- and long-term. Post-treatment residual protection is not provided by any of the processes. Thus, environmental control, facility and collection management are crucial factors in the continued success of any treatment once collections have been returned to storage. Additionally, administrative and operational requirements will play a role in the decision to select a specific process.

Clearly, prevention of infestation must be the primary goal of an institution. Through the use of an integrated management programme, populations of pests resident in most libraries can be effectively controlled. When infestations do occur, the nonchemical disinfestation processes offer a variety of options for the safe and effective treatment of collections. Further research is needed to fully confirm their effectiveness and usefulness for library application.

In the past, the effects and effectiveness of various pesticides especially fumigants, were not given appropriate and full evaluation prior to their use in libraries, as well as in archives and museums. Fortunately, it appears that this will not be the case with these nonchemical treatment processes. The current level of activity in research, testing and practical application points to the broad recognition of the need for comprehensive examination of these new treatment approaches. Such commitment will help to ensure that their development and implementation are carried out with a sufficient understanding of the associated benefits and risks.

9.0   GLOSSARY

ACCLIMATION Physiological adjustment that an organism exhibits to change in its immediate environment.

ACTINOMYCETES Bacteria with a characteristic filamentous branching shape that causes an infectious disease known as actinomycosis.

ACUTE Means sudden or brief. An acute exposure is a short-term exposure (minutes, hours or days). An acute health effect is an effect that develops either immediately or a short time after exposure.

ANAEROBIC Organism that can grow in the absence of atmospheric oxygen.

ANOXANT Agent that causes oxygen deficiency in the blood. Condition of such severity/duration as to result in permanent damage.

CARCINOGEN A substance which can cause cancer.

CHILL-COMA TEMPERATURE The temperature at which insects become inactive and unable to acclimate.

CHRONIC Means long-term or prolonged. A chronic exposure is a long-term exposure. A chronic health effect is an effect that appears months or years after an exposure.

DESICCANT A compound that promotes the loss of moisture.

EMERGENCE The adult insect leaving the pupal case or the last nymphal skin.

FREEZE AVOIDANCE In insects, a survival strategy demonstrated by freeze-sensitive insects exposed to low temperatures.

FREEZE RESISTANT Term applied to those insects that demonstrate freeze avoidance.

FREEZE SENSITIVE In insects, the lack of tolerance to formation of ice in the body fluid.

FREEZE TOLERANCE In insects, the ability to tolerate ice formation in the body fluid at temperatures equal to or below their supercooling capacity.

FREEZE-DRYING A type of dehydration for removing water from wet materials such as books. Materials are first frozen and then exposed to a vacuum, so that the water (ice) vapourizes in the vacuum (sublimes) without passing through the liquid state.

FUMIGANT Chemical substance that kills pests while in a gaseous state. Based on physical properties at room temperature there are three types: gaseous, liquid and solid.

FUMIGATION CHAMBER An air-tight enclosure where fumigants are used to eradicate insects and fungi. Some chambers can produce a vacuum.

FUNGUS Any of a group of thallophytic plants (phylum Thallophyta), mainly characterized by the absence of chlorophyll.

GRAY The Gray is the international unit for the measurement of radiation (absorbed dose unit). The more useful unit is the kGy (kilo Gray), 1 Gy = 0.001 kGy. Still in common use is an older unit of measurement called the rad from radiation absorbed dose (1Gy = 100 rad).

INSECT Class (Insecta) of the phylum Arthropoda, the largest taxonomic division of the animal kingdom, characterized by a body divided into segments and a hard, horny external covering called an exo-skeleton.

INSECTICIDE A type of pesticide that kills or interferes with the life cycle of insects, and is used to reduce or control insect populations. Most often used are either natural or synthetic organic compounds.

kGy Stands for Kilo Gray. See **GRAY**.

LARVAE The immature stages, between the egg and the pupa, of insects exhibiting complete metamorphosis.

LD_{50} Stands for lethal dose, where the dose of a chemical kills one half (50%) of the animal species (most often rats or mice) tested. The chemical may be given to the animals by mouth, by painting on the skin, by injection, etc. The LD_{50} value obtained is identified as the LD_{50} (oral), LD_{50} (dermal), etc. as appropriate. Where the chemical is mixed into the air which the test animals breathe or inhale, the result obtained is called an LC_{50} (for lethal concentration).

LC_{50} See LD_{50}.

METAMORPHOSIS A process in insects of periodic moulting where growth proceeds to the adult stage. The stages of complete metamorphosis are egg, larva, pupa and adult. The stages of incomplete metamorphosis are egg, larva, nymph and adult.

MUTAGEN A substance that can cause changes in the DNA of cells (mutations).

NYMPH An immature stage, after hatching, of an insect that does not have a pupal stage.

OXYGEN ABSORBER Substance that absorbs oxygen chemically. It is contained in a small bag like a desiccant and is widely used by the food industry for inclusion in packaging to maintain the original quality of the food.

PEL Stands for Permissible Exposure Limit. The U.S. Occupational Safety and Health Administration PEL is the eight hour time-weighted average legally enforceable standard.

PESTICIDE Any substance or mixture of substances designed to prevent, control, repel, kill or destroy any pest ie. insects, fungi, rodents, bacteria, etc.

pH Measure of the effective acidity or alkalinity of an aqueous solution, expressed as the negative logarithm of the hydrogen-ion concentration. A scale numbered from 0 to 14 is used. 7.0 is the neutral point. pH lower than 7.0 indicates acidity, while pH higher than 7.0 indicates alkalinity.

PHEROMONE Chemicals that are secreted by insects in order to modify the behaviour of other insects of the same species. These include sex attractants, feeding regulators, territory markers and others.

POLYMERIZATION The process of forming a polymer by combining large numbers of chemical units or monomers into long chains.

ppm Abbreviation for parts per million. It is a common unit of concentration of gases or vapour in air.

PRESELECTION Culling or sorting out materials which cannot be safely treated, or must be treated in groups so that they can be subjected to different treatment cycles/parameters.

PUPA The stage between the larva and the adult in insects exhibiting complete metamorphosis.

RESISTANCE The ability of pests to avoid or mitigate the effects of toxic pesticides or other adverse conditions such as extreme temperatures. The basis of resistance may be physical, physiological or behavioural.

SCIENTIFIC NAME A Latinized name, universally adopted, for a species or sub-species. The scientific name of a species consists of the generic and specific name and the name of the describer of the species. That of a sub-species consists of generic, specific, and sub-specific names and the name of the describer. Scientific names, except for the describer's name, are printed in italics. For example, *Blatta orientalis* (Linnaeus), known as the common or oriental cockroach.

SILICA GEL A colloidal form of silica available in the form of highly absorbent granules, and used as a dehumidifier. It is chemically inert, non-toxic, non-deliquescent, dimensionally stable and non-corrosive.

STEL Stands for Short Term Exposure Limit. It is the 15 minute maximum exposure limit recommended by the American Conference of Governmental Industrial Hygienists.

SUPERCOOLED Term applied to an insect that remains unfrozen below its freezing point.

SUPERCOOLING TEMPERATURE Temperature at which spontaneous freezing occurs in a supercooled system.

TERATOGEN A substance that can cause birth defects.

TLV Stands for Threshold Limit Value. It is the 8 hour time-weighted average exposure limit recommended by the American Conference of Governmental Industrial Hygienists. TLVs are adopted by some governments as their legal limits.

TOXICITY Toxicity is the ability of a substance to cause harmful health effects. Descriptions of toxicity (low, moderate, severe, etc.) depend on the amount needed to cause an effect or the severity of that effect.

10.0 REFERENCES

THE ABBEY NEWSLETTER. 1984. Gamma Radiation. *The Abbey Newsletter* 8(2):25,28.

THE ABBEY NEWSLETTER. 1984. More About Gamma Rays. *The Abbey Newsletter* 8(4):53-54.

THE ABBEY NEWSLETTER. 1986. Gamma Radiation Approval Seen. *The Abbey Newsletter* 10(1):12.

THE ABBEY NEWSLETTER. 1987. The AIC Meeting in Vancouver. *The Abbey Newsletter* 11(4):54.

THE ABBEY NEWSLETTER. 1990. B & G Bubble for Fumigation with Inert Gases. *The Abbey Newsletter* (14)8:148.

THE ABBEY NEWSLETTER. 1990. Oxygen Scavenger Retards Deterioration, Kills Bugs. *The Abbey Newsletter* 14(1):5.

THE ABBEY NEWSLETTER. 1990. The "Ageless" Project at CCI. *The Abbey Newsletter* 14(4):66.

THE ABBEY NEWSLETTER. 1991. NARA Tests Shrink-Wrapping of Bound Volumes. *The Abbey Newsletter* 15(7):105.

ABE, Y. and Y. KONDOH. 1989. Oxygen Absorbers. In *Controlled Atmosphere/Modified Atmosphere Vacuum Packaging of Foods,* ed. A. Brody. Trumbull, Connecticut: Food and Nutrition Press. 149-158.

ALI NIAZEE, M. 1971. The Effect of Carbon Dioxide Alone or in Combination on the Mortality of *Tribolium castaneum* (Herbst) and *T. confusum. Journal of Stored Food* 7:243-252.

ALLSOPP, D. 1985. Biology and Growth Requirements of Moulds and Other Deteriogenic Fungi. *Journal of the Society of Archivists* 7(8):530-533.

ALPERT, G.D. and L.M. ALPERT. 1988. Integrated Pest Management: A Program for Museum Environments. In *A Guide to Museum Pest Control,* eds. L.A. Zycherman and J.R. Schrock. Washington, D.C.: Foundation of the American Institute for Conservation of Historic and Artistic Works and Association of Systematics Collections. 169-176.

ANNIS, P.C. 1987. Towards a Rational Controlled Atmosphere Dosage Schedule: A Review of Current Knowledge. In *Proceedings of the 4th International Conference on Stored-Product Protection,* ed. E. Donahaye and S. Novarro. Tel Aviv. 126-148.

ARAI, H. and H. MORI. 1980. Studies on the Long-Term Conservation of Cultural Properties. Part 1 : Using Biaxially Oriented Polyvinylalcohol Film Bags to Prevent the Biodeterioration of Cultural Properties. *Scientific Papers on Japanese Antiques and Arts Crafts* 25:89-107. (In Japanese with English summary)

AREVAD, K. 1975. Control of Dermestid Beetles by Refrigeration. In *Danish Pest Infestation Laboratory Annual Report, 1974.* Lyngby, Denmark: The Laboratory. 41.

AREVAD, K. 1980. Dermestid Beetles: Control by Refrigeration. In *Danish Pest Infestation Laboratory Annual Report, 1979.* Lyngby, Denmark: The Laboratory. 64-65.

ARNEY, J.S. and L.B. POLLACK. 1980. The Retention of Organic Solvents in Paper. *Journal of the American Institute for Conservation* 19(2):69-74.

ART HAZARDS NEWS. 1990. NTP [National Toxicology Program] Criteria. *Art Hazards News* 13(6):2.

B & G EQUIPMENT COMPANY. 1989. *Operation and Instruction Manual for B & G Mini Fumigation Bubble - Developed by Rentokil.* Plumsteadville, Pennsylvania: B & G Equipment Co.

B & G EQUIPMENT COMPANY. n.d. *Mini Fumigation Bubble.* Plumsteadville, Pennsylvania: B & G Equipment Co.

BABIN, A. 1990. Dichlorvos Carcinogenicity Update. *Art Hazards News* 13(6):1-2.

BABIN, A. 1991. Uses, Hazards and Precautions of Phosphine. *Art Hazards News* 14(4):1.

BAER, N.S. and M.H. ELLIS. 1988. Conservation Notes on Thymol Fumigation. *The International Journal of Museum Management and Curatorship* 7:185-188.

BAILEY, S.W. and H.J. BANKS. 1974. The Use of Controlled Atmospheres for the Storage of Grain. In *Proceedings of the 1st International Working Conference on Stored Product Entomology.* Savannah, Georgia: Permanent Committee of the International Conference on Stored Product Protection. 362-374.

BAILEY, S.W. and H.J. BANKS. 1980. A Review of Recent Studies of the Effects of Controlled Atmospheres on Stored Product Pests. In *Controlled Atmosphere Storage of Grains,* ed. J. Shejbal. Amsterdam: Elsevier. 101-118.

BAKER, M.T., H.D. BURGESS, N.E. BINNIE, M.R. DERRICK and J.R. DRUZIK. 1990. Laboratory Investigation of the Fumigant Vikane. In *ICOM Committee for Conservation: 9th Triennial Meeting, Dresden, German Democratic Republic, 26-31 August, 1990, Preprints*, ed. K. Grimstead, Vol. 2. Marina del Rey, California: The Getty Conservation Institute. 804-811.

BALLARD, J.B. and R.E. GOLD. 1982. Ultrasonics: No Effect on Cockroach Behaviour. *Pest Control* 50(6):24,26.

BALLARD, M.W. and N.S. BAER. 1986. Ethylene Oxide Fumigation: Results and Risk Assessment. *Restaurator* 7(4):143-168.

BANKS, H.J. 1979. Recent Advances in the Use of Modified Atmospheres for Stored Product Pest Control. In *Proceedings of the 2nd International Working Conference on Stored Product Entomology*. Ibadan, Nigeria. 198-217.

BANKS, H.J. 1984. Current Methods and Potential Systems for Production of Controlled Atmospheres for Grain Storage. In *Controlled Atmosphere and Fumigation in Grain Storages*, eds. B.E. Ripp et al. Amsterdam: Elsevier. 523-542.

BANKS, H.J. 1984. Modified Atmosphere and Hermetic Storage - Effects on Insect Pests and the Commodity. In *Proceedings of the Australian Development Assistance Course on the Preservation of Stored Cereals*, eds. B.R. Champ and E. Highley. Canberra, Australia: CSIRO Division of Entomology. 521-532.

BARD, C.C. 1986. Biodeterioration of Photographs. In *Biodeterioration 6*. Papers presented at the 6th International Biodeterioration Symposium, Washington, D.C., August, 1984, eds. S. Barry and D.R. Houghton. London: CAB International Mycological Institute and The Biodeterioration Society. 379-382.

BARTON, L.V. 1949. Biological Effects of Freezing. *Refrigeration Engineering* 57:145-147.

BAUR, F.J., ed. 1984. *Insect Management for Food Processing and Storage*. St. Paul, Minnesota: American Association of Cereal Chemists.

BAYNES-COPE, A.D. and T.J. COLLINGS. 1980. Technical Note: Some Specifications for Materials and Techniques Used in the Conservation of Archives. *Journal of the Society of Archivists* 6(6):384-386.

BAYNES-COPE, A.D. and D. ALLSOPP. 1986. Observations on Mould Growth in Small Libraries. In *Biodeterioration 6*. Papers presented at the 6th International Biodeterioration Symposium, Washington, D.C., August, 1984, eds. S. Barry and D.R. Houghton. London: CAB International Mycological Institute and The Biodeterioration Society. 382-385.

BELL, B.M. and E.M. STANLEY. 1981. Survey of Pest Control Procedures in Museums. In *Pest Control in Museums: A Status Report (1980)*, eds. S.R. Edwards, B.M. Bell and M.E. King. Lawrence, Kansas: Association of Systematics Collections, University of Kansas. 11-4, Appendix G.

BELLO, S.J. and D.M. HALTON. 1986. *What is an LD$_{50}$?* Hamilton, Ontario: Canadian Centre for Occupational Health and Safety.

BELYAKOVA, L.A. 1960. Gamma-Radiation as a Disinfecting Agent for Books Infected with Mold Spores. *Microbiologiya* 29(5):762-765. (In Russian)

BLACKSHAW, S.M. and V.D. Daniels. 1979. The Testing of Materials for Use in Storage and Display in Museums. *The Conservator* 3:16-19.

BOAL, G.C. 1990. Blast Freezing the Berkeley Law Library Infestation. In *The 1990 Book and Paper Group Annual*, comp. R. Espinosa, Vol. 9. Washington, D.C.: Book and Paper Group of the American Institute for Conservation of Historic and Artistic Works. 17-28.

BOLT, R.O., and J.G. CARROLL, eds. 1963. *Radiation Effects on Organic Materials.* London and New York: Academic Press.

BONETTI, M., F. GALLO, G. MAGAUDDA, C. MARCONI and M. MONTANARI. 1979. Essais sur l'utilisation des rayons gammas pour la stérilization des matériaux libraires. *Studies in Conservation* 24(2):59-68. (In French)

BORAIKO, A.A. 1981. The Indomitable Cockroach. *National Geographic* 159(1):130-142.

BRANDT, A.-C. and A.J. BERTEAUD. 1987. Séchage par microondes pour la restauration de documents de papier en feuille ou en cahier. *Studies in Conservation* 32(1):14-24. (In French)

BRANDT, C.A.E. 1983. Planning an Environmentally Benign Fumigator Freeze Dryer for the Provincial Archives of Manitoba. *The American Institute for Conservation of Historic and Artistic Works, Preprints of Papers Presented at the Eleventh Annual Meeting, Baltimore, Maryland, 25-29 May, 1983.* Washington, D.C.: AIC. 1-7.

BREZNER, J. 1988. Protecting Books from Living Pests. In *TAPPI Proceedings - 1988 Paper Preservation Symposium*. Atlanta, Georgia: TAPPI Press. 65-68.

BREZNER, J. and P. LUNER. 1989. Nuke 'Em! Library Pest Control Using a Microwave. *Library Journal* (September):60-63.

BROKERHOF, A.W. 1989. *Control of Fungi and Insects in Objects and Collections of Cultural Value: "A State of the Art".* Amsterdam: Central Research Laboratory for Objects of Art and Science.

BROKERHOF, A.W. 1989. *Proposal for Research on the Application of Several Alternatives to Ethylene Oxide Fumigation to Control Insects and Fungi in Objects and Collections of Cultural Value.* Amsterdam: Central Research Laboratory for Objects of Art and Science.

BROWN-GORT, A. 1991. *Personal Communication* (Columbia University), April 11, 1991.

BRUCE, J. and L. McGREGOR. 1976. Technical Notes. *Archives and Manuscripts* 6(6):250.

BUTTERFIELD, F.J. 1986. Gamma-Irradiation as a Fungicide for Watercolour Drawings. In *The Institute of Paper Conservation, 10th Anniversary Conference, New Directions in Paper Conservation, 14-18 April 1986, Oxford, England. Conference Notes.* Comp., A. Howell. Leigh, Worcestershire, England: The Institute of Paper Conservation. F1.

BUTTERFIELD, F.J. 1987. The Potential Long-Term Effects of Gamma Radiation on Paper. *Studies in Conservation* 32(4):181-191.

CANADIAN CENTRE FOR OCCUPATIONAL HEALTH AND SAFETY. 1991. *Substitutes: Considerations for Selection.* Document 91/00831. Hamilton, Ontario: Canadian Centre for Occupational Health and Safety.

CANTWELL, G.E., G.J. TOMPKINS, and P. N. WATSON. 1973. Control of the German Cockroach with Carbon Dioxide. *Pest Control* 41(3):40-41,48.

CARLSON, J. 1992. *Personal Communication* (H.F. Dupont Winterthur Museum, January 23, 1992).

CASEY, P. and S. WALSTON. 1980. Systems for the Control of Pests. *ICCM Bulletin* 6(1):31-35.

CCH CANADIAN LIMITED. 1991. *Canadian Product Law Guide* (formerly Canadian Product Safety Guide). Don Mills, Ontario: CCH Canadian Limited.

CENTER FOR SAFETY IN THE ARTS. 1988. Chart of Fumigant Hazards. In *A Guide to Museum Pest Control,* eds. L.A. Zycherman and J.R. Schrock. Washington, D.C.: Foundation of the American Institute for Conservation of Historic and Artistic Works and Association of Systematics Collections. 127-134.

CHAMBERLAIN, W.R. 1982. Fungus in the Library. *Library & Archival Security* 4(4):35-55.

CHAMBERLAIN, W.R. 1987. A New Approach to Treating Fungus in Small Libraries. In *Biodeterioration Research I.* Proceedings of the First Pan-American Biodeterioration Society Annual Meeting. Washington, D.C., July, 1986, eds. G. C. Llewellyn and C.E. O'Rear. New York and London: Plenum Press. 323-327.

CHAPMAN, R.F. 1982. *The Insects: Structure and Function.* 3rd ed. Cambridge: University Press.

CHAPPAS, W.J. and N. McCALL. 1986. The Use of Ionizing Radiation in Disinfestation of Archival and Manuscript Materials. In *Biodeterioration 6.* Papers presented at the 6th International Biodeterioration Symposium. Washington, D.C., August, 1984, eds. S. Barry and D.R. Houghton. London: CAB International Mycological Institute and The Biodeterioration Society. 370-373.

CHENGFA, F., T. KAIZEN, Z. YUNLU, G. SACHAN, W. ZHENGFU and X. JIAFANG. 1988. The Gamma-Ray Radiation Preservation Technology for Files and Books. *Radiation and Physical Chemistry* 31(4-6):757-759.

CHILD, R.C. 1988. Fumigation: A New Direction? In *UKIC Preprints, 30th Anniversary Conference, United Kingdom Institute of Conservation.* London: UKIC. 101-103.

CHILD, R. C. 1991. Fumigation and the Rentokil 'Bubble'. *Library Conservation News* 32(July): 1-3.

CHILD, R.C. and D.B. PINNIGER. 1987. Insect Pest Control in U.K. Museums. In *Recent Advances in the Conservation and Analysis of Artifacts,* comp. J. Black. London: University of London, Institute of Archaeology, Summer Schools Press. 303-307.

CHONG QUEK, L., M. RAZAK, and M.K. BALLARD. 1990. Pest Control for Temperate vs. Tropical Museums: North America vs. Southeast Asia. In *ICOM Committee for Conservation: 9th Triennial Meeting, Dresden, German Democratic Republic, 26-31 August, 1990, Preprints,* ed. K. Grimstad, Vol. 2. Marina del Rey, California: The Getty Conservation Institute. 817-820.

CLARK, LLOYD. 1991. *Personnal Communication* (Maine State Archives), April 11, 1991.

COOKE, R.C. 1977. *Fungi, Man and his Environment.* New York: Longman.

COWAN, R.S. 1980. News of Herbarium Disinfestation of Dried Specimens at Kew. *Taxonomy* 29:198.

CRAIG, R. 1986. Alternative Approaches to the Treatment of Mould Biodeterioration - An International Problem. *The Paper Conservator* 10:27-30.

CRISAFULLI, S. 1980. Herbarium Insect Control with a Freezer. *Brittonia* 32(2):224.

CUNHA, G. and D.G. CUNHA. 1971. *Conservation of Library Materials: A Manual and Bibliography on the Care, Repair and Restoration of Library Materials.* 2nd ed. Vol. 1, Metuchen, N.J.: The Scarecrow Press.

CUNHA, G. M. 1977. An Evaluation of Recent Developments for the Mass Drying of Books. In *Preservation of Paper and Textiles of Historic and Artistic Value*, ed. J.C. Williams. Advances in Chemistry Series 164. Washington, D.C.: American Chemical Society. 95-104.

CZERWINSKA, E. and R. KOWALIK. 1979. Microbiodeterioration of Audiovisual Collections. Part 1. Protection of Audiovisual Records Against Destructive Microflora. Part 2. Microbial Problems in Photographic Print Collections. *Restaurator* 3(1-2):63-80.

DALLEY, J. 1990. *Personal Communication* (Provincial Archives of Manitoba, February 1, 1990.

DANIELS, V. and B. BOYD. 1986. The Yellowing of Thymol in the Display of Prints. *Studies in Conservation* 31(4):156-158.

DAVIS, M. 1985. Preservation Using Pesticides: Some Words of Caution. *Wilson Library Bulletin* (February):386-388,431.

DAVIS, M.B. 1984. Least Toxic Pest Control for Libraries. *The IPM Practitioner* 6(10):7-9.

DAVIS, R. and E.G. JAY. 1983. An Overview of Modified Atmospheres for Insect Control. *Association of Operative Millers Bulletin* (March):4026-4029.

DAWSON, J.E. 1981. Ethylene Oxide Fumigation. *IIC-CG Newsletter* 7(2):8-11.

DAWSON, J.E. 1983. Ethylene Oxide Fumigation: A New Warning. *ACA Bulletin* 8(3):10-13.

DAWSON, J. E. 1986. Effects of Pesticides on Museum Materials: A Preliminary Report. In *Biodeterioration 6*. Papers presented at the 6th International Biodeterioration Symposium, Washington, D.C., August, 1984, eds. S. Barry and D.R. Houghton. London: CAB International Mycological Institute and The Biodeterioration Society. 350-354.

DAWSON, J.E. 1986. Preventive Measures: Fumigation. In *Proceedings of An Ounce of Prevention*. A Symposium on Disaster Contingency Planning for Information Managers in Archives, Libraries and Record Centres, Toronto, 7-8 March 1985, ed. N. Willson. Toronto: Toronto Area Archivists Group Foundation. 54-63.

DAWSON, J.E. 1988. The Effects of Insecticides on Museum Artifacts and Materials. In *A Guide to Museum Pest Control*, eds. L.A. Zycherman and J.R. Schrock. Washington, D.C.: Foundation of the American Institute for Conservation of Historic and Artistic Works and Association of Systematics Collections. 135-150.

DeCANDIDO, R. 1988. Out of the Question - Fast Fires. *Conservation Administration News* 35:17,27.

DeCANDIDO, R. 1989. Out of the Question - Some Nukes. *Conservation Administration News* 36:22.

DeCESARE, K.B.J. 1990. Safe Nontoxic Pest Control for Books. *The Abbey Newsletter* 14(1):16.

DEAN, A.E. and K. TOWER, eds. 1991. *Fire Protection Guide on Hazardous Materials*. 10th ed. Quincy, Massachusetts: National Fire Protection Association.

DERRICK, M.R., H.D. BURGESS, M.T. BAKER and N.E. BINNIE. 1990. Sulfuryl Fluoride (Vikane): A Review of its Use as a Fumigant. *Journal of the American Institute for Conservation* 29(1):77-90.

DERSARKISSIAN, M. and M. GOODBERRY. 1980. Experiments with Non-Toxic Fungal Agents. *Studies in Conservation* 25(1):28-36.

DeTASSIGNY, C. and BROUQUI, M. 1978. Adaption à la désinfection de la momie de Ramses II du procédé de radiostérilization gamma. In *ICOM Committee for Conservation, 5th Triennial Meeting, Zagreb, Yugoslavia, 1978, Preprints.* Paris: ICOM. 17/4/1/ - 17/4/10. (In French)

DHAWAN, S. 1987. *Microbial Deterioration of Paper Material: A Literature Review.* Lucknow, India: National Research Library for Conservation of Cultural Property.

DREISBACH, R.H. and W.O. ROBERTSON. 1987. *Handbook of Poisoning Prevention, Diagnosis and Treatment.* Norwalk, Connecticut: Appleton and Lange.

DRUZIK, J.R. 1992. *Personal Communication* (The Getty Conservation Institute, January 29, 1992).

DVORIASHINA, Z.P. 1979. Some Regularities of Book-Storage Contamination by Insects. *Restaurator* 3(3):109-116.

DVORIASHINA, Z.P. 1987. Biodamage Protection of Book Collections in the USSR. *Restaurator* 8:(4)182-188.

DVORIASHINA, Z.P. 1988. The Smirnov Beetle as a Pest in Libraries. *Restaurator* 9(2):63-81.

EBELING, W. 1975. *Urban Entomology.* California: University of California, Division of Agricultural Sciences.

EBELING, W., C.F. FORBES and S. EBELING. 1989. Heat Treatment for Powderpost Beetles. *The IPM Practitioner* 11(9):1-4.

EDELSON, Z. 1978. Peabody Notebook. Beinecke Library vs the Deathwatch Beetles: Charles Remington Prescribes Deep-Freezing. *Discovery* 13(1):45-46.

EDWARDS, S.R., B.M. BELL and M.E. KING, eds. 1981. *Pest Control in Museums: A Status Report (1980)*. Lawrence, Kansas: Association of Systematics Collections, University of Kansas.

ELLIS, M.H. 1987. *The Care of Prints and Drawings*. Nashville, Tennessee: American Association for State and Local History. Appendix 3.

ENTWISTLE, R.M. and J. PEARSON. 1988. Rentokil Bubble. *Conservation News* 37:11-12.

ENTWISTLE, R.M. and J. PEARSON. 1989. Workshop Notes - Rentokil Bubble, Results of Test. *Conservation News* 38:7-9.

FENN, J. 1989. Fumigation with Hydrogen Phosphide "Phostoxin" at the Royal Ontario Museum. In *Proceedings of the 14th Annual IIC-CG Conference, May 27-30, 1988, Toronto, Ontario, Canada,* ed. J. Wellheiser. Toronto: Toronto Area Conservation Group of the International Institute for Conservation of Historic and Artistic Works-Canadian Group. 115-123.

FENN, J. 1990. Health and Safety: Textile Fumigation with Phosphine. *Textile Conservation Newsletter* 19(Fall):15-18.

FERRO, F. 1978. Freezer Blasts Beinecke Bookworms. *Connecticut Libraries* 20:34-38.

FISCHER, D.J. 1977. Conservation Research: Fumigation and Sterilization of Flood-Contaminated Library, Office, Photographic, and Archival Materials. In *Preservation of Paper and Textiles of Historic and Artistic Value,* ed. J.C. Williams. Advances in Chemistry Series 164. Washington, D.C.: American Chemical Society. 139-148.

FISCHER, D.J. 1977. Conservation Research: Use of Dielectric and Microwave Energy to Thaw and Dry Frozen Library Materials. In *Preservation of Paper and Textiles of Historic and Artistic Value,* ed. J.C. Williams. Advances in Chemistry Series 164. Washington, D.C.: American Chemical Society. 124-138.

FISCHER, D.J. 1977. Simulation of Flood for Preparing Reproducible Water-Damaged Books and Evaluation of Traditional and New Drying Methods. In *Preservation of Paper and Textiles of Historic and Artistic Value,* ed. J.C. Williams. Advances in Chemistry Series 164. Washington, D.C.: American Chemical Society. 105-123.

FLORIAN, M.-L. 1978. Biodeterioration of Museum Objects: An Ecological Approach to Control and Prevention. *Museum Round Up* 72: 35-43.

FLORIAN, M.-L. 1986. Letter to the Editor re Haines and Kohler article JAIC 25(1986):49-55. *Journal of the American Institute for Conservation* 25(2):109.

FLORIAN, M.-L. 1986. The Freezing Process - Effects on Insects and Artifact Materials. *Leather Conservation News* 3(1):1-13,17.

FLORIAN, M.-L. 1987. Methodology Used in Insect Pest Surveys in Museum Buildings; A Case History. In *ICOM Committee for Conservation: 8th Triennial Meeting, Sydney, Australia, 6-11 September, 1987, Preprints,* ed. K. Grimstad, Vol. 3. Marina del Rey, California: The Getty Conservation Institute. 1169-1174.

FLORIAN, M.-L. 1987. The Effect on Artifact Materials of the Fumigant Ethylene Oxide and Freezing used in Insect Control. In *ICOM Committee for Conservation: 8th Triennial Meeting, Sydney, Australia, 6-11 September, 1987, Preprints,* ed. K. Grimstad, Vol. 1. Marina del Rey, California: The Getty Conservation Institute. 199-208.

FLORIAN, M.-L. 1988. Ethylene Oxide Fumigation: A Literature Review of the Problems and Interactions with Materials and Substances in Artifacts. In *A Guide to Museum Pest Control,* eds. L.A. Zycherman and J.R. Schrock. Washington, D.C.: Foundation of the American Institute for Conservation of Historic and Artistic Works and Association of Systematics Collections. 151-158.

FLORIAN, M.-L. 1989. Integrated System Approach to Insect Pest Control: An Alternative to Fumigation. In *Proceedings of Conservation in Archives: International Symposium, Ottawa, Canada, May 10-12, 1988.* Ottawa: International Council on Archives. 252-262.

FLORIAN, M.-L. 1990{a}. Freezing for Museum Insect Pest Eradication. *Collection Forum* 6(1):1-7.

FLORIAN, M.-L. 1990{b}. *Personal Communication* (Royal British Columbia Museum, March 20, 1990).

FLORIDA ENTOMOLOGIST. 1988. Student Symposium: Alternatives to Chemical Control of Insects. *Florida Entomologist* 71(4): 505-580.

FORBES, C.F. and W. EBELING. 1987. Update: Use of Heat for Elimination of Structural Pests. *The IPM Practitioner* 9(8):1-5.

FRANKIE, G.W. and C.S. KOEHLER. 1978. *Perspectives in Urban Entomology.* New York: Academic Press.

GAGNON, M. and M. BEAULIEU. 1985. *Étude de faisabilité sur la stérilization des livres ou documents au moyen des rayons gamma.* Unpublished report. Laval, Québec: Centre de recherches en sciences appliqués à l'alimentation de l'Institut Armand Frappier, Université du Québec. (In French)

GALLO, F. 1975. Recent Experiments in the Field of Disinfection of Book Materials. In *ICOM Committee for Conservation: 4th Triennial Meeting, Venice, 13-18 October 1975, Preprints.* Paris: ICOM. 75/15/7-1 - 75/15/7-21.

GALLO, F. 1985. *Biological Factors in Deterioration of Paper.* Trans. S. O'Leary. Rome: ICCROM.

GENTRY, J.W. 1984. Inspection Techniques. In *Insect Management for Food Storage and Processing,* ed. F.J. Baur. St Paul, Minnesota: American Association of Cereal Chemists. 33-42.

THE GETTY CONSERVATION INSTITUTE NEWSLETTER. 1988. Vikane Holds Potential as a Museum Fumigant. *The Getty Conservation Institute Newsletter* 3(1):6.

GIBSON, J.A. and D. REAY. 1982/3. Drying Rare Books Soaked by Water: A Harwell Experiment. *The Paper Conservator* 10:28-34.

GILBERG, M. 1989. AGELESS Oxygen Scavenger. *AICCM Newsletter* 32(1):6.

GILBERG, M. 1989. Inert Atmosphere Fumigation of Museum Objects. *Studies in Conservation* 34(2):80-82.

GILBERG, M. 1990. Inert Atmosphere Disinfestation Using Ageless Oxygen Scavenger. In *ICOM Committee for Conservation: 9th Triennial Meeting, Dresden, German Democratic Republic, 26-31 August, 1990, Preprints,* ed. K. Grimstead, Vol. 2. Marina del Rey, California: The Getty Conservation Institute. 812-816.

GILBERG, M. 1991. The Effects of Low Oxygen Atmospheres on Museum Pests. *Studies in Conservation* 36(2):93-98.

GILBERG, M. and A. BROKERHOF. 1991. The Control of Insect Pests in Museum Collections: The Effects of Low Temperatures on *Stegobium Paniceum* (Linneaus), The Drugstore Beetle. *Journal of the American Institute for Conservation* 30(2):197-201.

GILLET, M. and C. GARNIER. 1989. The Use of Microwaves for Drying Flood Damaged Photographic Materials. In *Topics in Photographic Preservation,* comp. R.E. Siegel, Vol. 3. Washington, D.C.: American Institute for Conservation of Historic and Artistic Works Photographic Materials Group. 46-51.

GOSSELIN, R.E., R.P. SMITH AND H.C. HODGE. 1984. *Clinical Toxicology of Commercial Products.* 5th ed. Baltimore: Williams and Wilkins.

GOULD, G.W. 1988. Control of Microbial Growth through the Exclusion of Air. In *Biodeterioration 7*. Papers presented at the 7th International Biodeterioration Symposium. Cambridge, U.K., September, 1987, eds. D.R. Houghton, R.N. Smith and H.O.W. Eggins. London and New York, Elsevier Applied Science. 529-534.

GRATTAN, D. 1988. "Ageless" and "Ageless Eye". *CCI Newsletter* June:7.

GRATTAN, D. 1990. *Ageless Project Status - March 1990*. Unpublished report. Ottawa: Canadian Conservation Institute.

GREATHOUSE, G.A. and C.J. WESSEL. 1954. *Deterioration of Materials. Causes and Preventive Techniques*. New York: Reinhold.

GREEN, L. and V. DANIELS. 1987. Investigation of the Residues Formed in the Fumigation of Museum Objects Using Ethylene Oxide. In *Recent Advances in the Conservation and Analysis of Artifacts*, comp. J. Black. London: University of London, Institute of Archaeology, Summer Schools Press. 309-313.

GREEN, L. and R. GOLDSTRAW. 1988. Packaging Materials. *Conservation News* 37:11.

GUSTAFSON, R.A. et al. 1990. Fungicidal Efficacy of Selected Chemicals in Thymol Cabinets. *Journal of the American Institute for Conservation* 29(2):153-168.

HAINES, J.H. and S.A. KOHLER. 1986. An Evaluation of Ortho-Phenyl Phenol as a Fungicidal Fumigant for Archives and Libraries. *Journal of the American Institute for Conservation* 25(2):49-55.

HALL, D.W. 1981. Microwave: A Method to Control Herbarium Insects. *Taxonomy* 30(4):818-819.

HALL, L.E. 1989. The Effects of Thymol on Paper, Pigments and Media. In *Papers Presented at the Fourteenth Annual Art Conservation Training Programs Conference: May 4-5, 1988, Art Conservation Department, Buffalo State College*. Buffalo: Buffalo State College, Art Conservation Department. 77-84.

HANUS, J. 1985. Gamma Radiation for Use in Archives and Libraries. *The Abbey Newsletter* 9(2):34.

HARRISON, J.R. 1989. Conservation Materials and their Potential Toxicity: The Science of Toxicology. In *Proceedings of Conservation in Archives: International Symposium, Ottawa, Canada, May 10-12, 1988*. Ottawa: International Council on Archives. 263-272.

HASTINGS, P. 1992. *Personal Communication* (Houston Museum, January 23, 1992).

HEIM, W.R., F. FLIEDER and J. NICOT. 1968. Combatting the Moulds Which Develop on Cultural Property in Tropical Climates. In *The Conservation of Cultural Property with Special Reference to Tropical Conditions.* Paris: UNESCO. 41-52.

HICKIN, N. 1985. *Bookworms: The Insect Pests of Books.* London: Sheppard Press.

HICKIN, N. 1985. *Pest Animals in Buildings - A World Review.* New York: Longman.

HIGHLAND, H.A. 1984. Insect Infestation of Packages. In *Insect Management for Food Processing and Storage,* ed. F.J. Baur. St. Paul, Minnesota: American Association of Cereal Chemists. 311-320.

HILLMAN, D. and V. THORP. 1989. Museum Pest Management: The Collection Inspection Room. In *Proceedings of the 14th Annual IIC-CG Conference, May 27-30, 1988, Toronto, Ontario, Canada,* ed. J. Wellheiser. Toronto: Toronto Area Conservation Group of the International Institute for Conservation of Historic and Artistic Works - Canadian Group. 101-106.

HOLMES, J. 1991. *Personal Communication* (National Archives of Canada), December 3, 1990.

HORAKOVA, H. and F. MARTINEK. 1984. Disinfection of Archive Documents by Ionizing Radiation. *Restaurator* 6(3-4):205-216.

HURLOCK, E.T., B.E. LLEWELLING and L.M. STABLES. 1979. Microwaves Can Kill Insect Pests. *Manufacture* 8:37-39.

IMHOLTE, T.J. 1984. *Engineering for Food Safety and Sanitation - A Guide to the Sanitary Design of Food Plants and Food Plant Equipment.* Crystal, Minnesota: Technical Institute of Food Safety.

JAY, E.G. 1971. *Suggested Conditions and Procedures for Using Carbon Dioxide to Control Insects in Grain Storage Facilities.* ARS Report 51-46. Washington, D.C.: U.S. Department of Agriculture, Agriculture Reserve Service.

JAY, E. 1980. *Methods of Applying Carbon Dioxide for Insect Control in Stored Grain.* U.S. Department of Agriculture/Science and Education Administration Advances in Agricultural Technology, Southern Series, No. 13.

JAY, E. 1984. Recent Advances in the Use of Modified Atmospheres for the Control of Stored-Product Pests. In *Insect Management for Food Processing and Storage,* ed. F.J. Baur. St. Paul Minnesota: American Association of Cereal Chemists. 239-254.

JAY, E.G., R.T. ARBOGAST and G.C. PEARMAN. 1971. Relative Humidity: Its Importance in the Control of Stored-Product Insects with Modified Atmospheric Gas Concentrations. *Journal of Stored Product Research* 7:325-329.

JAY, E.G. and W. CUFF. 1981. Weight Loss and Mortality of Three Stages of *Tribolium castaneum* (Herbst) when Exposed to Four Modified Atmospheres. *Journal of Stored Product Research* 17:117-124.

JAY, E.G. and G.C. PEARMAN. 1971. Susceptibility of Two Species of *Tribolium* (Coleoptera: Tenebrionidae) to Alterations of Atmospheric Gas Concentrations. *Journal of Stored Product Research* 7:181-186.

KEENEY JR., N. H. and J.W. WALKINSHAW. 1990. The Effects of Radiation on the Strength of Medical Packaging Papers. *TAPPI Journal* (October):233-236.

KENJO, T. 1977. Effects of Insecticidal and Fungicidal Agents on Materials of Cultural Properties. *Scientific Papers on Japanese Antiques and Arts Crafts* 19-20:83-87. (In Japanese with English summary)

KENJO, T. 1980. Studies on the Long-Term Conservation of Cultural Properties. Part 1, (2) Effects of Different Concentrations of Oxygen on Pigments Used for Cultural Properties. *Scientific Papers on Japanese Antiques and Arts Crafts* 25:103-107. (In Japanese with English summary)

KENJO, T. 1985. The Use of Nikka Pellets and Japanese Tissue Made Plain. *The International Journal of Museum Management and Curatorship* 4(1):65-72.

KETCHAM, J.D. 1983. *The Use of Chemical Pesticides in the Care of Museum Collections.* Kingston, Ontario: Queen's University.

KETCHAM, J.D. 1984. *Investigations into Freezing as an Alternative Method of Disinfecting Proteinaceous Artifacts: The Effects of Subfreezing Temperatures on* Dermestes maculatus Degeer *(Coleoptera: Dermestidae). Masters Thesis.* Kingston, Ontario: Queen's University.

KOESTLER, R. J. and E.D. SANTORRO. 1991. Biodeterioration in Museums - Observations. In *Biodeterioration Research 3.* New York: Plenum Publishing. (In press)

KOZULINA, O.V. and Z.P. BARYSHNIKOVA. 1978. The Use of Synthetic Insecticides Against the Vermin in Books. *Restaurator* 2(3-4)191-202.

KOWALIK, R. 1979. Some Remarks of a Microbiologist on Protection of Library Materials Against Insects. *Restaurator* 3(4):117-122.

KOWALIK, R. 1980. Microbiodeterioration of Library Materials Part 1: Chapters 1-3. *Restaurator* 4(2):99-114.

KOWALIK, R. 1980. Microbiodeterioration of Library Materials Part 2: Chapter 4; Microbiodecomposition of Basic Organic Library Materials. *Restaurator* 4(3-4):135-219.

KOWALIK, R. 1984. Microbiodeterioration of Library Materials Part 2: Chapters 5-9; Microbiodecomposition of Auxiliary Materials. *Restaurator* 6(1-2): 61-115.

KRUTH, L.M. 1989. Paper Conservation Update: Bleaching and Fumigation. *The Abbey Newsletter* 13(5):90-92.

LAWSON, P. 1988. Freezing as a Means of Pest Control: An Experimental Note. *Library Conservation News* 20:6.

LECLERC, F. 1989. Effets des rayons gamma sur le papier: état de la question. In *Patrimoine culturel et altérations biologiques: actes des journées d'êtude de la SFFIC, Poitiers, 17-18 novembre 1988.* Marseilles: Section française de l'Iinstitut international de conservation. 91-95. (In French)

LEY, F.J. 1988. The Control of Microorganisms Using Ionising Radiation. In *Biodeterioration 7.* Papers presented at the 7th International Biodeterioration Symposium. Cambridge, U.K., September, 1987, eds. D.R. Houghton, R.N. Smith and H.O.W. Eggins. London and New York, Elsevier Applied Science. 523-528.

LILLI DI FRANCO, M., M.T. LOCURCIO RASOLA and T. HACKENS, eds. 1985. *The Conservation of Library and Archive Property,* European Postgraduate Course 2, Rome, April, 1980. Ravello, Italy: European University Center for the Cultural Heritage.

LIM, G., T.K. TAN and A. TOH. 1989. The Fungal Problem in Buildings in the Humid Tropics. *International Biodeterioration* 25:27-37.

MAKES, F. 1984. Damage to Old Bindings in the Skokloster Library. *Skokloster Studies* 71:33-57.

MALLIS, A. 1990. *Handbook of Pest Control: The Behaviour, Life History, and Control of Household Pests.* eds. K. Story and D. Moreland. 7th ed. Cleveland: Franzak & Foster.

MAW, J.M. and R.N. SMITH. 1986. Monitoring Microbial Activity on Surfaces. In *Biodeterioration 6.* Papers presented at the 6th International Biodeterioration Symposium, Washington, D.C., August 1984, eds. S. Barry and D.R. Houghton. London: CAB International Mycological Institute and The Biodeterioration Society. 154-160.

McCALL, N. 1983. Gamma Radiation as a Sterilant. *Society of American Archivists Newsletter* (November):6.

McCALL, N. 1984. Gamma Radiation. *The Abbey Newsletter* 8(2):25.

McCALL, N. 1985. Ionizing Radiation as an Exterminant: A Case Study. *Conservation Administration News* 23:1-2,20,23.

McCALL, N. 1990. *Personal Communication* (Johns Hopkins Medical Institutions, January 9, 1990).

McCOMB, R.E. 1983. Three Gaseous Fumigants. *The Abbey Newsletter* 7(1):12.

McCRADY, E. 1989. TAPPI Symposium: Full Report. *The Abbey Newsletter* 13(1):1-2, 4.

McGIFFIN JR., R.F. 1985. *A Current Status Report on Fumigation in Museums and Historical Agencies.* Technical Report 4. Nashville: American Association for State and Local History.

MEISTER SR., R., ed. 1991. *Farm Chemicals Handbook.* Willoughby, Ohio: Meister Publishing Co.

MITSUBISHI GAS CHEMICAL COMPANY, INC. 1987. *Oxygen Absorber "Ageless": A New Age in Food Preservation.* Tokyo: Mitsubishi Gas Chemical Company.

MULLEN M.A. and R.T. ARBOGAST. 1979. Time-Temperature-Mortality Relationships for Various Stored-Product Insect Eggs and Chilling Times for Selected Commodities. *Journal of Economic Entomology* 72(4):476-478.

MULLEN, M.A. and R.T. ARBOGAST. 1984. Low Temperatures to Control Stored Product Insects. In *Insect Management for Food Processing and Storage,* ed. F.J. Baur. St. Paul, Minnesota: American Association of Cereal Chemists. 255-264.

MULLEN, M. A. and R.T. ARBOGAST. n.d. *Low Temperatures to Control Stored-Product Insects.* Savannah: Georgia: Stored-Product Insects Research and Development Laboratory, Agricultural Research Service.

NAGIN, G. and M. McCANN. 1982. *Thymol and o - Phenyl Phenol: Safe Work Practices.* Data Sheet, Centre for Occupational Hazards. New York, Centre for Occupational Hazards.

NAIR, S.M. 1986. Biodeterioration of Museum Collections by Dermestid Beetles, With Particular Reference to Tropical Countries. In *Biodeterioration 6.* Papers presented at the 6th International Biodeterioration Symposium, Washington, D.C., August, 1984, eds. S. Barry and D.R. Houghton. London: CAB International Mycological Institute and The Biodeterioration Society. 337-343.

NAKAMURA, H. and J. HOSHINO. 1983. Techniques for the Preservation of Food by Employment of an Oxygen Absorber. In *Sanitation Control for Food Sterilizing Techniques.* Tokyo: Sanyu Publishing Co. Chapter XII.

NATIONAL INSTITUTE FOR OCCUPATIONAL SAFETY AND HEALTH. 1990. *Registry of Toxic Effects of Chemical Substances*. Washington, D.C.: National Technical Information Service.

NATIONAL RESEARCH LIBRARY FOR CONSERVATION OF CULTURAL PROPERTY. 1989. *International Conference on Biodeterioration of Cultural Property Abstracts, February 1989*. Lucknow, India: National Research Library for Conservation of Cultural Property.

NAVARRO, S. and E.G. JAY. 1987. Application of Modified Atmospheres for Controlling Stored Grain Insects. In *Stored Products Pest Control. Proceedings of a Symposium at Reading, U.K., 1987*, BCPC Monograph No. 37, ed. T.J. Lawson. 229-236.

NELSON, S.O. 1962. Radiation Processing in Agriculture. *Transactions of the American Society of Agricultural Engineers* 5: 20-25,30.

NELSON, S.O. 1966. Electromagnetic and Sonic Energy for Insect Control. *Transactions of the American Society of Agricultural Engineers* 9:389-405.

NELSON, S.O. 1973. Insect-Control Studies with Microwaves and Other Radiofrequency Energy. *Bulletin of the Entomological Society of America* 19:157-163.

NELSON, S.O. and W.K. WHITNEY. 1960. Radio Frequency Electrical Fields for Stored Grain Insect Control. *Transactions of the American Society of Agricultural Engineers* 3:133-137,144.

NESHEIM, K. 1984. The Yale Non-toxic Method of Eradicating Book-Eating Insects by Deep-freezing. *Restaurator* 6(3-4):147-164.

NETWORK NEWS. 1990. Atmospheric Gas Fumigation. *Network News* 3(1):8.

NEWMAN, W. 1989. Sources of Information on Health and Safety for Archivists and Conservationists. In *Proceedings of Conservation in Archives: International Symposium, Ottawa, Canada, May 10-12, 1988*. Ottawa: International Council on Archives. 273-279.

NEWTON, J. 1988. Insects and Packaging - A Review. *International Biodeterioration* 24:175-187.

NOACK, G. 1990. *Personal Communication* (Yale University), January 4, 1990.

NYBERG, S. 1987. *The Invasion of the Giant Spore*. Solinet Preservation Leaflet No. 5. Atlanta, Georgia: SOLINET.

NYBERG, S. 1988. Out of the Question - How Effective is Ortho-phenyl phenol...? *Conservation Administration News* 33:14-15,23.

NYUKSHA, J.P. 1979. Biological Principles of Book Keeping Conditions. *Restaurator* 3(3):101-108.

NYUKSHA, J.P. 1980. Biodeterioration and Biostability of Library Materials. *Restaurator* 4(1):71-77.

NYUKSHA, J.P., O.A. GROMOV, J.V. POKROVSKAJA and M.E. SALTYKOV. 1990. Mass Processing of Documents for Fungi Contamination Control. In *ICOM Committee for Conservation: 9th Triennial Meeting, Dresden, German Democratic Republic, 26-31 August, 1990, Preprints*, ed. K. Grimstad, Vol. 2. Marina del Rey, California: The Getty Conservation Institute. 478-481.

NYUKSHA, YU.P. 1983. Some Special Cases of Biological Deterioration of Books. *Restaurator* 5(3-4):177-182.

OGUCHI, Y., S. TAZUKI and J. FUKAMI. n.d. *Insecticidal Effect of the Oxygen Absorber "Ageless" on Insects Injurious to Stored Grains.* Japan: The Institute of Physical and Chemical Research, Laboratory of Insect Toxicology.

OLKOWSKI, W. and H. OLKOWSKI. 1983. *Integrated Pest Management for Park Managers: A Training Manual.* Washington, D.C.: U.S. National Park Service.

OCCUPATIONAL SAFETY AND HEALTH ADMINISTRATION, U.S. DEPARTMENT OF LABOUR. 1990. *OSHA Regulated Hazardous Substances: Health, Toxicity, Economic and Technological Data.* Park Ridge, New Jersey: Noyes Data Corp.

OSMUN, J.V. 1984. Insect Pest Management and Control. In *Insect Management for Food Processing and Storage*, ed. F.J. Baur. St. Paul, Minnesota: American Association of Cereal Chemists. 17-24.

PAGE, W.J. and W.G. MARTIN. 1978. Survival of Microbial Films in the Microwave Oven. *Canadian Journal of Microbiology* 24:1431-1433.

PARDUE, D. 1987. Integrated Pest Management in the United States Parks Service. In *ICOM Committee for Conservation: 8th Triennial Meeting, Sydney, Australia, 6-11 September, 1987, Preprints*, ed. K. Grimstad, Vol. 3. Marina del Rey, California: The Getty Conservation Institute. 1183-1187.

PARKER, A.E. 1989. The Freeze-Drying Process: Some Conclusions. *Library Conservation News* 23:4-6,8.

PARKER, T.A. 1987. Integrated Pest Management for Libraries. In *Preservation of Library Materials*. Conference held at the National Library of Austria, Vienna, April 7-10, 1986, ed. M. A. Smith, IFLA Publications 41. Munich, London, New York, Paris: K.G. Saur. 103-123.

PARKER, T.A. 1988. *Study on Integrated Pest Management for Libraries and Archives*. Paris: General Information Programme and UNISIST, UNESCO.

PARKER, T.A. 1988. Pesticide Terminology. In *A Guide to Museum Pest Control*, eds. L.A. Zycherman and J.R. Schrock. Washington, D.C.: Foundation of the American Institute for Conservation of Historic and Artistic Works and Association of Systematics Collections. 123-126.

PARKER, T.A. 1991{a}. *The Practical Application of Pheromone Traps in Libraries and Archives*. Paper presented at the International Seminar on Research in Preservation and Conservation, Columbia University, New York, May 25, 1991. Sponsored by the International Federation of Library Associations and Institutions, International Council on Archives and Columbia University School of Library Service Conservation Education Programs. (Unpublished)

PARKER, T.A. 1991{b}. *Personal Communication* (Pest Control Services Inc., September 15, 1991).

PATTON, R. and J.W. CREFFIELD. 1987. The Tolerance of Some Timber Insect Pests to Atmospheres of Carbon Dioxide in Air. *International Pest Control* 29(1):10-12.

PAVON FLORES, S.C. 1975-76. Gamma Radiation as Fungicide and its Effects on Paper. *Bulletin of the American Institute for Conservation* 16(1): 15-44.

PAYNE, N.M. 1926. Freezing and Survival of Insects at Low Temperature. *Quarterly Review of Biology* 1:270-282.

PELTZ, P. and M. ROSSOL. 1983. *Safe Pest Control Procedures for Museum Collections*. New York: Centre for Occupational Hazards.

PETHERBRIDGE, G. and J.M. HARRINGTON, eds. 1981. Safety and Health in the Paper Conservation Laboratory. 1980/81. *The Paper Conservator* 5 and 6.

PINNIGER, D. 1989. *Insect Pests in Museums*. London: Institute of Archaeology Publications.

POSTLETHWAITE, A.W. 1987. Fumigation, Choice of Fumigant and Design of Facility. In *ICOM Committee for Conservation: 8th Triennial Meeting, Sydney, Australia, 6-11 September, 1987, Preprints*, ed. K. Grimstad, Vol. 3. Marina del Rey, California: The Getty Conservation Institute. 1189-1196.

POSTLETHWAITE, A.W. 1991. *Achieving Integrated Pest Eradication with Heightened Sensitivities to Collection Safety and Human Toxicity.* Paper presented at the International Seminar on Research in Preservation and Conservation, Columbia University, New York, May 25, 1991. Sponsored by the International Federation of Library Associations and Institutions, International Council on Archives and Columbia University School of Library Service Conservation Education Programs. (Unpublished)

RAMIÈRE, R. 1981. *Protection de l'environnement culturel par les techniques nucléaires. Conférence organisée par IAEA Grenoble, France, 28 sept. - 20 oct. 1981.* Grenoble, France: IAEA. 255-270. (In French).

RAYNES, P. 1986. Insects and Their Control in the Library. *Conservation Administration News* 27:4,24-25.

REAGAN, B.M. 1982. Eradication of Insects from Wool Textiles. *Journal of the American Institute for Conservation* 21(2):1-34.

REAGAN, B.M., J.H. CHIAO-CHENG and N.J. STREIT. 1980. Effects of Microwave Radiation on the Webbing Clothes Moth, Tineola bisselliella (Hum.) and Textiles. *Journal of Food Protection* 43:658-663.

RESIDORI, L. and P. RONCI. 1986. Preliminary Study of the Use of Ethylene Oxide for the Sterilization and Disinfestation of Books and Documents. *The Paper Conservator* 10:49-54.

RIPP, B.E., ed. 1984. *Controlled Atmosphere and Fumigation in Grain Storages.* Proceedings of an International Symposium, Perth, Australia, April, 1983. Amsterdam: Elsevier.

ROGGIA, S. 1989. Letters - No need to "nuke 'em". *Library Journal* (December):8.

RUSSELL, I.S. 1988. Federal Statutes and Regulations Governing the Use of Pesticides and an Annotation of Federal Pesticide Regulations. In *A Guide to Museum Pest Control,* eds. L.A. Zycherman and J.R. Schrock. Washington, D.C.: Foundation of the American Institute for Conservation of Historic and Artistic Works and Association of Systematics Collections. 9-49.

RUST, M.K. and J. KENNEDY, 1991. *Status Report: Feasibility of Using Modified Atmospheres to Control Insect Pests in Museums.* Paper presented at the International Seminar on Research in Preservation and Conservation, Columbia University, New York, May 25, 1991. Sponsored by the International Federation of Library Associations and Institutions, International Council on Archives and Columbia University School of Library Service Conservation Education Programs. (Unpublished)

112

RUST, M.K. and J. KENNEDY, 1992. *Status Report: Feasibility of Using Modified Atmospheres to Control Insect Pests in Museums*. Marina del Rey, California: The Getty Conservation Institute. (In preparation)

RUTHERFORD, L.O. 1987. Cryobibliotherapy. *The New Library Scene* 6(3):1,5-9.

SADURSKA, I. and R. KOWALIK. 1975. Some Tests Upon Microbioresistance of Adhesives Used in Archive and Library Materials Conservation. In *ICOM Committee for Conservation: 4th Triennial Meeting, Venice, 13-18 October 1975, Preprints*. Paris: ICOM. 75/15/18-1 - 75/15/18-10.

SALT, R.W. 1936. *Studies on the Freezing Process in Insects: Doctoral Thesis*. University of Minnesota.

SALT, R.W. 1950. Time as a Factor in the Freezing of Under-Cooled Insects. *Canadian Journal of Research* 28(D):285-291.

SALT, R.W. 1958. Application of Nucleation Theory to the Freezing of Supercooled Insects. *Journal of Insect Physiology* 2:178-188.

SALT, R.W. 1961. Principles of Insect Cold-Hardiness. *Annual Review of Entomology* 6:55-74.

SALT, R.W. 1970. Analysis of Insect Freezing Temperature Distributions. *Canadian Journal of Zoology* 48(2):205-208.

SANDERS, S. 1987. Effects of CO_2 Fumigation on pH. In *ICOM Committee for Conservation: 8th Triennial Meeting, Sydney, Australia, 6-11 September, 1987, Preprints*, ed. K. Grimstad, Vol. 3. Marina del Rey, California: The Getty Conservation Institute. 945-946.

SARKAR, N.N. 1985-87. A New Sterilization Process and Standardization of Lethal Doses for Insect Eggs by Vacuum Fumigation Chamber. *Conservation of Cultural Property in India* 18-20:86-89.

SAX, N.I. 1984. *Dangerous Properties of Industrial Materials*. New York: Van Nostrand, Reinhold.

SCHOFIELD, E. K. and S. CRISAFULLI. 1980. A Safer Insecticide for Herbarium Use. *Brittonia* 31(1):58-62.

SHEJBAL, J., ed. 1980. *Controlled Atmosphere Storage of Grains: Developments in Agricultural Engineering 1*. Amsterdam: Elsevier.

SHEPPARD, K.O. 1984. Heat Sterilization (Superheating) as a Control for Stored-Grain Pests in A Food Plant. In *Insect Management for Food Processing and Storage,* ed. F. J. Baur. St. Paul, Minnesota: American Association of Cereal Chemists. 193-200.

SMITH, C.P. and J. NEWTON. 1991. *Carbon Dioxide: The Fumigant of the Future.* Paper presented at the International Seminar on Research in Preservation and Conservation, Columbia University, New York, May 25, 1991. Sponsored by the International Federation of Library Associations and Institutions, International Council on Archives and Columbia University School of Library Service Conservation Education Programs. (Unpublished)

SMITH, R.D. 1984. Fumigation Dilemma: More Overkill or Common Sense. *The New Library Scene* 3(6):1,5-6.

SMITH, R.D. 1985. Background, Use and Benefits of Blast Freezers in the Prevention and Extermination of Insects. In *Biodeterioration 6.* Papers presented at the 6th International Biodeterioration Symposium, Washington, D.C., August 1984, eds. S. Barry and D.R. Houghton. London: CAB International Mycological Institute and The Biodeterioration Society. 374-379.

SMITH, R.D. 1985. The Use of Redesigned and Mechanically Modified Commercial Freezers to Dry Water-Wetted Books and Exterminate Insects. *Restaurator* 6(3-4):165-190.

SMITH, R.D. 1986. Fumigation Quandary: More Overkill or Common Sense? *The Paper Conservator* 10:46-48.

SMITH, R.D. 1990. *Personal Communication* (Wei T'o Associates Inc., January 2, 1990).

SOCIETY OF CHEMICAL INDUSTRY. 1966. *Microbial Deterioration in the Tropics.* Papers presented at The Microbiology Group Symposium, London, April, 1965. S.C.I. Monograph No.23. London: Society of Chemical Industry.

STANSFIELD, G. 1985. Pest Control - A Collection Management Problem. *Museums Journal* 85(2):97-99.

STEWART, E. 1983. *The Use of Low Temperatures in Eradicating Insects Destructive to Library Materials.* Unpublished paper prepared for Columbia University School of Library Service Course, Protection and Care of Record Materials.

STEWART, E. 1988. Freeze Disinfestation of the McWilliams Collection. *Conservation Administration News* 32:10-11,25.

STONE, J.L. and J.A. EDWARDS. 1988. Dichlorvos in Museums: An Investigation into its Effects on Various Materials. In *A Guide to Museum Pest Control*, eds. L.A. Zycherman and J.R. Schrock. Washington, D.C. Foundation of the American Institute for Conservation of Historic and Artistic Works and Association of Systematics Collections. 159-168.

STORY, K.O. 1985. *Approaches to Pest Management in Museums.* Suitland, Maryland: Conservation Analytical Laboratory, Smithsonian Institution.

STRANG, T.J.K. 1991. *Dealing with Vertebrate Pests in Museums. Technical Bulletin No. 13.* Ottawa: Canadian Conservation Institute.

STRANG, T.J.K. 1991. *Guidelines for Museum Pest Control - Low Temperature. C.C.I. Note 3/2.* Ottawa: Canadian Conservation Institute. (In preparation)

STRANG, T.J.K. 1992{a}. *Personal Communication* (Canadian Conservation Institute, January 29, 1992).

STRANG, T.J.K. 1992. *Solving Museum Insect Problems: Nonchemical Control. Technical Bulletin No. 14.* Ottawa: Canadian Conservation Institute. (In preparation)

STRANG, T.J.K. rev. 1992 (Unpublished manuscript by J.E. DAWSON). *Solving Museum Insect Problems: Chemical Control. Technical Bulletin No. 15.* Ottawa: Canadian Conservation Institute. (In preparation)

STRANG, T.J.K. and J.E. DAWSON. 1991. *Controlling Museum Fungal Problems. Technical Bulletin No. 12.* Ottawa: Canadian Conservation Institute.

STRASSBURG,R. 1978. The Use of Fumigants in Archival Repositories. *American Archivist* 41:25-36.

STRZELCZYK A.B. and J. KUROCZKIN. 1989. Studies on the Microbial Degradation of Ancient Leather Bookbindings. Part 2. *International Biodeterioration* 25:39-47.

SWARTZBURG, S. 1987. Cryobibliotherapy. *Conservation Administration News* 30:12.

SZCZEPANOWSKA, H. 1986. Biodeterioration of Art Objects on Paper. *The Paper Conservator* 10:31-39.

SZCZEPANOWSKA, H. 1989. Assessing the Activity of Fungal Growth on Art Objects with a View to Possible Fumigation. *Conservation Administration News* 37:12.

SZCZEPANOWSKA, H. and LOVETT JR., C.M. 1988. Fungal Stains on Paper. In *The Conservation of Far Eastern Art*, Preprints for the Contributions to the Kyoto Congress, 19-23 September 1988, eds. Mills, J.S., P. Smith and K. Yamasaki. London: International Institute for Conservation of Historic and Artistic Works. 13-14.

SZENT-IVANY, J.J.H. 1968. Identification and Control of Insect Pests. In *The Conservation of Cultural Property with Special Reference to Tropical Conditions*. Paris, UNESCO. 53-70.

TENHOOR, J. 1991. *Personal Communication* (Newberry Library), April 21, 1991.

THOMSON, G. 1986. *The Museum Environment*. Second edition. London: Butterworths in association with The International Institute for Conservation of Historic and Artistic Works.

TILTON, E.W. and H.H. VARDELL. 1981. An Evaluation of a Pilot-Plant Microwave Vacuum Drying Unit for Stored Product Insect Control. *Journal of the Georgia Entomological Society* 17:126-132.

TOSKINA, I.N. 1978. Wood Pests in Articles and Structures and Pest Control in Museums. In *ICOM Committee for Conservation: 5th Triennial Meeting, Zagreb, Yugoslavia, 1978, Preprints*. Paris: ICOM. 78/13/2/1-17/13/2/10.

URBAN, J. and P. JUSTA. 1986. Conservation by Gamma Radiation: The Museum of Central Bohemia in Roztoky. *Museum* 151:165-167.

URBAN, J., I. SANTAR, J. SEDLACKOVA and J. PIPOTA. 1978. Use of Gamma Radiation for Conservation Purposes in Czechoslovakia. In *ICOM Committee for Conservation: 5th Triennial Meeting, Zagreb, Yugoslavia, 1978, Preprints*. Paris: ICOM 17/4/1-17/4/10.

VALENTIN, N. 1986. Biodeterioration of Library Materials: Disinfection Methods and New Alternatives. *The Paper Conservator* 10:40-45.

VALENTIN, N. 1990. Insect Eradication in Museums and Archives by Oxygen Replacement, A Pilot Project. In *ICOM Committee for Conservation: 9th Triennial Meeting, Dresden, German Democratic Republic, 26-31 August, 1990, Preprints*, ed. K. Grimstad, Vol. 2. Marina del Rey, California: The Getty Conservation Institute. 821-823.

VALENTIN, N. 1991{a}. *Controlled Atmosphere for Insect Eradication in Library and Museum Collections*. Paper presented at the International Seminar on Research in Preservation and Conservation, Columbia University, New York, May 25, 1991. Sponsored by the International Federation of Library Associations and Institutions, International Council on Archives and Columbia University School of Library Service Conservation Education Programs. (Unpublished)

VALENTIN, N. 1991{b}. *Personal Communication* (Instituto de Conservación y Restauración, July 5, 1991).

VALENTIN, N. and F. PREUSSER. 1990. Insect Control by Inert Gases in Museums, Archives and Libraries. *Restaurator* 11(1): 22-33.

VALENTIN, N. and F. PREUSSER. 1991. Nitrogen for Biodeterioration Control of Museum Collections. In *Biodeterioration 3*. New York: Plenum Publishing. (In press)

VALENTIN, N., M. LIDSTROM and F. PREUSSER. 1990. Microbial Control by Low Oxygen and Low Relative Humidity Environment. *Studies in Conservation* 35(4):222-230.

VON ENDT, D.W. and W.C. JESSUP. 1986. In *Biodeterioration 6.* Papers presented at the 6th International Biodeterioration Symposium, Washington, D.C., August, 1984, eds. S. Barry and D.R. Houghton. London: CAB International Mycological Institute and The Biodeterioration Society. 332-337.

VORONINA, L.I., O.N. NAZAROVA and YU.P. PETUSHKOVA. 1980. Disinfection and Straightening of Parchment Damaged by Microorganisms. *Restaurator* 4(2):91-97.

VORONINA, L., O. NAZAROVA, U. PETUSHKOVA and N. REBRIKOVA. 1981. Damage of Parchment and Leather Caused by Microbes. In *ICOM Committee for Conservation: 6th Triennial Meeting, Ottawa, 1981. Preprints.* Paris: ICOM. 19/3/1 - 19/3/11.

WARD, P.R. 1976. *Getting the Bugs Out*, Museum Methods Manual No. 4. Victoria, B.C.: Friends of the Provincial Museum.

WARE, G.W. 1980. *Complete Guide to Pest Control - With and Without Chemicals.* Fresno, California: Thomson Publications.

WARREN, S. 1992. *Personal Communication* (National Museum of Science and Technology, January 23, 1992).

WATTERS, F.L. 1984. Potential of Ionizing Radiation for Insect Control in the Cereal Food Industry. In *Insect Management for Food Processing and Storage*, ed. F.J. Baur. St. Paul, Minnesota: American Association of Cereal Chemists. 265-278.

WEBB, E.A., C. PATTERSON, C.A. MEANEY and B. SNELGROVE. 1989. Integrated Pest Management at the Denver Museum Museum of Natural History. *Collection Forum* 5(2):52-59.

WEINSTEIN, F.R. 1984. A Psocid by Any Other Name...(Is Still a Pest). *Library & Archival Security* 6(1):57-63.

WEISS, R. 1988. Staying One Step Ahead of Their Six. *Science News* 134:22.

WEI T'O ASSOCIATES INC. 1984. *Wei T'o Book Dryer - Insect Exterminator Operation Manual*. Matteson, Illinois: Wei T'o Associates Inc.

WEI T'O ASSOCIATES INC. 1988. *Wei T'o Book Dryer - Insect Exterminator*. Matteson: Illinois: Wei T'o Associates Inc.

WESSEL, C.J. 1970. Environmental Factors Affecting the Permanence of Library Materials. In *Deterioration and Preservation of Library Materials*. The Thirty-fourth Annual Conference of the Graduate Library School, August 4-6, 1969, eds. H.W. Winger and R.D. Smith. Chicago and London: The University of Chicago Press. 39-84.

WHITEHEAD, D.L. and W.S. BOWERS, eds. 1983. *Natural Products for Innovative Pest Management*. Current Themes in Tropical Science Vol. 2. New York: Pergamon Press.

WIGGLESWORTH, V.B. 1972. *The Principles of Insect Physiology*. London: Chapman and Hall.

WILLIAMS S.L., C.A. HAWKS and S.G. WEBER. 1986. Considerations in the Use of DDVP Resin Strips for Insect Pest Control in Biological Research Collections. In *Biodeterioration 6*. Papers presented at the 6th International Biodeterioration Symposium, Washington, D.C., August, 1984, eds. S. Barry and D.R. Houghton. London: CAB International Mycological Institute and The Biodeterioration Society. 344-350.

WILLIAMS, S.L. and S.B. McLAREN. 1990. Modification of Storage Design to Mitigate Insect Problems. *Collection Forum* 6(1):27-32.

WILLIAMS, S.L. and E.A. WALSH. 1989. Effects of DDVP on a Museum Insect Pest. *Curator* 32(1):34-41.

WILLIAMS, S.L. and E.A. WALSH. 1989. Behaviour of DDVP in Storage Cases. *Curator* 32(1):41-49.

WILLIAMS, S.L., E.A. WALSH and S.G. WEBER. 1989. Effect of DDVP on Museum Materials. *Curator* 32(1):49-69.

WILSON, C. 1990. Moths, Moths and More Moths. *Museum Round Up* 152:1-3.

WINGER, H.W. and R.D. SMITH. 1970. *Deterioration and Preservation of Library Materials*. The 34th Annual Conference of the Graduate Library School, August, 1969. Chicago and London: The University of Chicago Press.

WINKS, R.G. and B.R. CHAMP. 1977. The Principles of Pest Control in Museums. In *Conservation in Australia*, ed. S. Walton. Sydney, Australia: Institute for Conservation of Cultural Material. 77-79.

WOOD LEE, M. 1988. *Prevention and Treatment of Mold in Library Collections with an Emphasis on Tropical Climates: A Ramp Study.* Paris: General Information Programme and UNISIST, UNESCO.

WORTHING, C.R. and S.B. WALKER, eds. 1987. *The Pesticide Manual: A World Compendium.* 8th ed. British Crop Protection Council, Lavenham: Lavenham Press.

YALE UNIVERSITY NEWS RELEASE. 1977. Yale Library Develops New Deep-Freeze Method to Kill Book-Eating Insects. *Yale University News Release.* No. 43. New Haven, Connecticut.

ZACHARIASSEN, K.E. 1985. Physiology of Cold Tolerance in Insects. *Physiological Review* 64(Oct):799-832.

ZAITSEVA, G.A. 1978. Dermestidae Beetles Injurious to Museum Objects and Protection Measures Against Them. In *ICOM Committee for Conservation: 5th Triennial Meeting, Zagreb, Yugoslavia, 1978, Preprints.* Paris: ICOM. 1-8.

ZAITSEVA, G.A. 1987. Chemical Measures of Protecting U.S.S.R. Museum Collections Against Keratin-Destroying Insects (Coleoptera, Dermestidae, Lepidoptera, Tineidae). In *ICOM Committee for Conservation: 8th Triennial Meeting, Sydney, Australia, 6-11 September, 1987, Preprints,* ed. K. Grimstad. Vol. 3. Marina del Rey, California: The Getty Conservation Institute. 1211-1214.

ZAITSEVA, G.A., K.P. ZABOTIN, A.I. KRAPANOV, I.J. PAVLINOV, P.D. FRAISHTAT and M.M. SHEMJAKIN. 1990. New Antifeedants for Pest Insects in Collections and Various Aspects of Their Use in Collections. In *ICOM Committee for Conservation: 9th Triennial Meeting, Dresden, German Democratic Republic, 26-31 August, 1990, Preprints,* ed. K. Grimstad, Vol. 2. Marina del Rey, California: The Getty Conservation Institute. 824-828.

ZYCHERMAN, L.A. and J.R. SCHROCK, eds. 1988. *A Guide to Museum Pest Control.* Washington, D.C.: Foundation of the American Institute for Conservation of Historic and Artistic Works and Association of Systematics Collections.

International Federation of Library Associations and Institutions

Series IFLA Publications

Edited by Carol Henry

Volume 54: Education and Training for Conservation and Preservation
Papers of an International Seminar on "Teaching of Preservation, Management for Librarians, Archivists and Information Scientists", sponsored by IFLA, FID and ICA. Vienna, April 11-13, 1986, with additional information sources
By Josephine Riss Fang
Edited by IFLA
With the assistance of Anna J. Fang
1991. VII, 113 pages. Hardbound
DM 58.00. IFLA members DM 43.50
ISBN 3-598-21782-X

Volume 55: Continuing Professional Education. An IFLA Guide Book
A Publication of the Continuing Professional Round Table (CPRT) of the International Federation of Library Associations and Institutions (IFLA)
Edited by Blanche Wools
Reports from the Fields edited by Miriam H. Tees
1991. X, 159 pages. Hardbound
DM 78.00. IFLA members DM 59.00
ISBN 3-598-21784-6

Volume 56: Reference Service for Publications of Intergovernmental Organizations
Papers from an IFLA workshop, Paris, August 1989. Section on Government Information and Official Publications, Section on Bibliography, Section on Social Science Libraries
Edited by Alfred Kagan
1991. VI, 158 pages. Hardbound
DM 68.00. IFLA member DM 51.00
ISBN 3-598-21785-4

Volume 57: Managing the Preservations of Serial Literature
Edited by Merrily A. Smith
1992. XI, 291 pages. Hardbound
DM 98.00. IFLA members DM 73.50
ISBN 3-598-21783-4

Volume 58: La Presse de la Liberté
Journée d'études organisée par le groupe de Travail IFLA sur les Journaux Paris le 24 août 1989
Seminar organised by the IFLA Working Group on Newspapers
Edited by Carol Henry
1991. IV, 123 pages. Hardbound
DM 68.00. IFLA members DM 51.00
ISBN 3-598-21786-2

K·G·Saur
München·Leipzig·London·New York·Paris

K·G·Saur Verlag · Ortlerstrasse 8 · Postfach 70 16 20 · D-8000 München 70 · Tel. (089) 7 69 02-0